Visionary Woman

Moved by Purpose

Not by Sight

A Timeless Message of Vision, Purpose, Hope, Tenacity, Resilience, Courage, Faith and True Leadership.

Created by Dr Sylvia Forchap-Likambi in collaboration with eight visionary women and world-class leaders.

Copyright ©2022 by

Dr Sylvia Forchap- Likambi

Dr Anikphe Oyedeji

Dr. Elizabeth Fon

Angela Preston

Neva Brooks

Blanka Volna

Thelma Birchall

Ellen Mandizvidza

Dr Bertille Nganwa

Softback: ISBN-13: 978-1-913266-09-7

Published in the United Kingdom in 2022 by Likambi Global Publishing Ltd

All rights reserved. No part of this book may be reproduced or transmitted in any form or by any means, electronic or mechanical, including photocopying, recording, or by an information storage and retrieval system – except by a reviewer who may quote brief passages in a review to be printed in a magazine or newspaper – without permission in writing from the copyright owner.

Other books by the Authors:

Personal & Professional Transformation and Success Planner: Your Blueprint to Success & Abundance in All Areas of Your Life – Parts one and two

ISBN-13: 978-1-913266-08-0

Unleash Your Authentic Identity: Unlock Your True Identity & Purpose

ISBN-13: 978-1-913266-95-0

Success Blueprint: Timeless Principles to Enable You to Identify & Accomplish True Success & Fulfilment in All Areas of Life

ISBN-13: 978-1-913266-98-1

Principles of Resolution: A Practical Step-by-Step Guide to Enable You to Identify, Set & Accomplish Your Goals

ISBN 10: 1543063780

ISBN13:9781543063783

Seven Powerful Strategies for Overcoming Life Challenges: Tested & Proven Life-Changing Keys

ISBN-13: 978-1-913266-02-8

ISBN-10: 1975669584

A Father's Tender and Compassionate Love: A Love so Tender, Compassionate, and Unconditional

ISBN 10: 1479772887/ ISBN 13: 9781479772889

ISBN 10: 1479772879 ISBN/ 13: 9781479772872

Riley in Memoriam, Anthology

ISBN 10: I-55606-099-2

Centered in Christ, Steadfast & Immovable

ISBN 13: 978-1-7320260-7-0

Opening Doors

ISBN-10: 1504945700

ISBN-13: 978-1504945707

The Keys to Success in Business

ISBN-10: 1524665452

ISBN-13: 978-152466545

Overcoming: Enforcing Your Victory in Christ

ISBN-13: 978-1-7391866-0-9

Upcoming books on the Visionary Woman Series by Dr Anikphe Oyedeji:

Visionary Woman: You Are God's Building

ISBN-13: 978-1-913266-16-5

Visionary Woman: You Are God's Garden

ISBN-13: 978-1-913266-17-2

TABLE OF CONTENTS

Dedication vii

Acknowledgements ix

Preface... xi

Introduction 1

Chapter One: The Power of Vision And Purpose 7

Chapter Two: We Are God's Handiwork................................... 27

Chapter Three: All In The Name.. 45

Chapter Four: The Art of Resilience 61

Chapter Five: Diamond Sharpens Diamond............................... 77

Chapter Six: Finding Myself... 95

Chapter Seven: Breaking Walls- Finding My Worth 111

Chapter Eight: Victory At Last.. 127

Chapter Nine: Story of A Life 147

Conclusion... 165

Authors' Biography 173

Dedication

This book is dedicated to visionary and purpose-driven women and leaders of unwavering faith and confidence – who are not moved by sight or fear, but by conviction and purpose. Be blessed and be inspired by the remarkable stories and inspirational journeys of tenacity, resilience, courage, faith, and true leadership of nine powerful visionary women and leaders from across the globe.

With love and gratitude,

Dr Sylvia Forchap-Likambi

Acknowledgements

My heartfelt gratitude goes to the incredibly powerful, tenacious, and purpose-driven visionary leaders and co-authors of this timeless manuscript, who believed in this vision and joined me in making it a reality.

To Dr Anikphe Oyedeji, Dr. Elizabeth Fon, Angela Preston, Neva Brooks, Blanka Volna, Thelma Birchall, Ellen Mandizvidza, and Dr Bertille Nganwa, it has been truly inspiring and a pleasure working with you all. Thank you for believing in me and this project, and for being an integral part of this contemporary manuscript.

To my wonderful family and team at Likambi Global Publishing, thank you for your support, devotion, and commitment throughout this journey and for working hard to ensure that this manuscript is published in such a short period of time.

Above all, I would like to express endless gratitude and honour to my Heavenly Father and Creator, for this vision and the provision to make it a reality! All Glory be to Him!

Preface

I vividly remember sitting in my bedroom one afternoon and working on one of my manuscripts for an upcoming book as all these inspirational thoughts flooded my mind. I had diverse inspiration and profound revelations on how I could better serve in my calling and impact more lives through my work and books. Then, like a flash of lightning, I thought to myself, *What about writing a book with other phenomenal visionaries and female leaders who share common principles on leadership, success, purpose, and life as a whole, like myself?* I thought this would be a brilliant and life-changing project and would definitely give birth to a timeless best-selling book that many women from diverse backgrounds and cultures could resonate with and draw wisdom and success principles from to live a purposeful and fulfilling life so that they may never give up in the face of challenges.

I thought about my vision for serving women. A deep conviction that someday, every female child worldwide would become aware of their authentic identity, worth, and value, and take full control of their lives regardless of their race, background, culture, religion, or the circumstances surrounding them. They will be able to make fundamental choices and decisions that will shape and determine their lives and destiny, and not let man or society shape and determine these for them. I was convinced in my spirit that the time is now and the place is here and that a ground-breaking project will help us accomplish part of that vision. With great excitement and enthusiasm, the Visionary Woman, moved by purpose and not by sight, was born and I stepped out and took the necessary steps to connect with the global visionaries and pioneers who were destined to become an integral part of this vision and project. Now here we are today, connecting with you from across the globe and sharing with you our stories and unique messages of tenacity, faith, and resilience.

We are nine powerful and diverse visionary women and global leaders with a unique message of hope, tenacity, courage, and resilience. Our goal is to share with you and our beloved readers our inspirational stories and journeys of tenacity, resilience, courage, faith, and true leadership, and to inspire you to remain hopeful and keep your eyes focused on your vision and dreams of a better life – no matter what. We desire to inspire and birth more visionary and purpose-driven leaders of unwavering faith and confidence – who are not moved by sight or fear – but by unwavering conviction and purpose.

Now, before you proceed any further into the transformational chapters of this book, I would like to take this opportunity to share with you a poem of mine that is close to my heart. It is a poem that will remind you of who you truly are and your worth.

This poem is dedicated to you, woman of valour and purpose!

Visionary Woman

A Woman's Splendour Revealed

There comes a time when the perception of a woman as a domestic slave, doormat, and sexual object is eradicated and her splendour is acknowledged and appreciated by the world.

The time is here, the time is now.

Let every man, nation, and continent in the world acknowledge and appreciate a woman's splendour and worth, regardless of her skin colour, religion, background, or circumstance.

A woman is a true reflection of the love and wisdom of our creator, God Almighty, who enables her with the unique attributes and potentials to recreate and give birth to life.

A Woman represents love, peace, endurance, kindness, gentleness, forgiveness, energy, and life. A woman is the mother of all men and nations; tiny and great, simple and complex, poor and rich, lost and found, humble and arrogant.

Her gentle love and tenderness, kind and forgiving nature enables her to love unconditionally and endure with patience the afflictions and bruises brought upon her body and soul by these same men and nations she conceived in her very own womb and gave birth to. Men and nations without her very own existence would be made void.

A woman is like mother earth; she upholds, bears and nourishes every seed planted into her and brings forth fruits of splendour and greatness. She is trampled upon and exploited for selfish desires, yet she is the foundation, home and food for all who trample upon her and exploit her.

Dr Sylvia Forchap-Likambi et al

A woman is the core of families, generations, nations, and the world. If only the world could sit back for an instant, gaze, and reflect upon her majesty, it would be evident just how powerless and void it would be without her existence.

A tiny little fetus she conceived in her womb, loved, nurtured, nourished, and protected from the harsh realities of the world. Her very own body was home, light, food, and drink for the tiny little vulnerable creature. Through sickness, fatigue, distress, and complications her whole being went, yet not for an instant did she think of terminating its life.

She held firm onto the tiny little creature within her womb with hope and life. She went on gradually, second by second, minute by minute, hour by hour, day by day, week by week and month by month, enduring, loving, and hoping, until it was the appointed time of travail and birth of the of the tiny little precious life within her, who represents generations, nations, and the world today.

The same world which has turned against her, used and abused her, yet she has never stopped loving, caring, and protecting it, not even for a moment. A mother's unconditional and true love.

Let every man, woman, nation, and the world lighten up and allow the burning flame of love, gentleness, kindness, and wisdom of a woman transform souls, nations, and the world.

In honour of every woman worldwide.

By Dr Sylvia Forchap Likambi

INTRODUCTION

I am honored and privileged to have such an incredible opportunity to collaborate with eight powerful visionary leaders and women of valour and tenacity to address beautiful people full of energy and strength like you. We are here to collectively remind you that you are beautifully and wonderfully made, uniquely and meticulously created for a definite purpose and destined for greatness. You are special, a true masterpiece, and endowed with great potential and abilities to impact our world— you should never let anyone tell you otherwise, or be led to believe otherwise.

Do not let a friend, teacher, parent, authority, or even yourself dare tell you that you are a failure or are of no use, because you are uniquely created for a unique purpose that only you could fulfill. In fact, you are the only one endowed with the attributes to fulfill this purpose or mission. Think about it this way, if your mission is not carried out by you to add value to humanity, it remains unaccomplished because no one else could dare to do it better than you.

Consequently, I am writing these introductory words before you step into the first chapters of this timeless manuscript to assure you that the future is bright and prosperous. You are very talented and equipped with all that you need to fulfil your purpose. Wake up and grasp your future, your life, your purpose. Reclaim the future, life, and identity that have been stolen from you by violence, distrust, frustration, despair, drugs, alcohol, abuse, etc. You have what it takes to be in perfect control of your life.

I say to you beloved and great mother of all nations – great and small - this is the time, the time is here, and the time is now. Wake up and possess that which rightfully belongs to you and has been stolen away from you. Arise and walk in your purpose. Step out and live your life, your dream, your vision, your future, a future full of hope and prosperity. A future only you have the ultimate authority and power to take back and live it in full.

I address you here today because you are at my heart. I feel a great need to step out and call you back on track if you have gone off track, to call you back to the path of hope and vision, because that is where you rightfully belong. I am here to call you back to the path of your God-given purpose. It is my duty, it is my purpose to do this, and above all, I love you so dearly like a sister, and I do not want to lose you out of despair, distrust, or a lack of hope and vision.

I know you might be thinking, *But you don't even know me, nor I you. How can you say you love me dearly like a sister? You do not know my life; you would not love my life for one second if only you knew who I really am.*

I stand by your side today through this manuscript to tell you this, beloved: I might not know you, or the life you live, or the mess you find yourself in, but the one thing I know for sure is this: you are unique and special, and endowed with great abilities to positively transform your circumstances and our world.

Your experiences, messes, circumstances, background, and beliefs are all part of what makes you different from me and hence, unique. The qualities and experiences that make you different and set you apart from me or the crowd are those very things that make you unique and special. The fact that you are different, unique, and special represents a testament of hope and victory to those who will go through similar challenges like you. I love these attributes about you. For I do not focus on the things I see in you currently (sight), for the things you and I currently see are subject to change and only temporary.

On the contrary, I choose to focus on the things I do not yet see in you, yet believe will come to pass in your life; for the things we do not see are eternal, they are permanent. Whatever challenges you might be going through at the moment (be it depression, abuse, violence, addiction, etc), it is not relevant for you to focus on that and use the situation to define you. I hereby beseech you to focus on your vision, the future, the good plans God has in store for you, for they are bright and prosperous. In everything, it is about you making a choice, life is all about choices; here is your time to choose to focus on your current situation (what you see) or on your future (your vision and purpose for living), which is full of hope and prosperity. I call on you to choose the latter; a future full of hope and prosperity.

My dear visionary friend and leader of tomorrow, once more I say, do not give up, if there is hope for me then there is surely hope for everyone. I stand here today and address you as a Black African woman from a "deprived" country in Africa, yet these attributes do not shape my personality and hold me back from thriving in my full potential. It doesn't matter where I come from, it doesn't matter what skin colour I have, it doesn't matter what my background or gender is.

When I look at myself, I do not see Black, I do not think of Africa, nor do I see woman; all I perceive is a beautiful, special, courageous, and unique creation of the Almighty God, who is endowed with great potentials and abilities to positively impact our world. These potentials are embedded within me and were placed within me at birth, and that is what I see… that is who I am.

Yet, I am very proud to be Black…to come from Cameroon (West Africa), and to be a woman, because these attributes make me unique. They were specifically assigned to me, because someone with such specifications was needed for my purpose to be fulfilled… my purpose of giving hope and life to the deprived, the oppressed, the lost, and the underprivileged. My background or disadvantages in life have been exploited as stepping stones to challenge me to excel into greater heights and fulfill my purpose.

Do not perceive the challenges and barriers that you face in life as stumbling blocks. Instead, use them as stepping stones to shape and prompt yourself into fulfilling your purpose of existence.

Do not be afraid to dream big, have great visions, and do all you can on your part to ensure they come to pass; so as to fulfill your purpose; and let no one tell you otherwise, because you were born to thrive, you were born for a purpose, to excel and not to be content in mediocrity.

I am not naïve to think that the path will be smooth and without obstacles, or that everyone around you will encourage you, cheer you up, and believe in you. No, far from it, in fact. I am aware of the endless obstacles, challenges, naysayers, critics, etc that you will encounter along your path to greatness! For this reason, I will close with some words of wisdom in dealing with these naysayers and critics— whenever they show up… which you could adopt from now on; what I term "the winner's mindset."

Overcoming Critics and Naysayers

The next time you meet people in life who try to discourage you or tell you that you cannot achieve your goals and dreams, ask them if they have ever successfully achieved similar dreams in their lifetime?

I bet their responses will be something like these: "we have all been there and know a lot of people too who have been there and tried so hard but failed," or "it is not that easy as you think, you know," "you need to be careful, else you might end up very disappointed," "you need this, you need that and that;" this list goes on and on to give you all the roadblocks needed for failure.

I bet so many of you have already come across such people in life. All those with such mindsets belong to a distinct category of people who make up what I refer to as the "losing team;" and so, have no better advice to give you, than the strategies and testimonials of losers. I therefore implore you to go to a winner the next time you intend to win a race; as you will be empowered with the knowledge and strategies to become a winner. For this reason, we have brought together ten powerful winners and visionaries from across the globe to share their journey and experience of victory with you.

No one says it's going to be an easy journey, yet it is the outcome that really matters to a winner, and that is where their focus lies. And because you are a champion, I therefore challenge you to redirect your focus.

Believe in your abilities, thrive, and succeed and watch yourself soar to greater heights and fulfill your life purpose. The winner's mindset is "I can do it," "I am well equipped," and ``I will do it regardless of the obvious obstacles and shortcomings I am faced with."

I hope you leave here empowered and with a winner's mindset.

CHAPTER ONE

THE POWER OF VISION AND PURPOSE

By Dr Sylvia Forchap-Likambi

"When you do not know who you are or what you want in life, there is a great tendency for you to eventually settle for a mediocre life! Therefore, to live an all-fulfilling and exceptional life, it is paramount that you go back to the basics of self-identification."

Dr Sylvia Forchap-Likambi

"The first step toward creating an improved future is developing the ability to envision it. VISION will ignite the fire of passion that fuels our commitment to do WHATEVER IT TAKES to achieve excellence. Only VISION allows us to transform dreams of greatness into the reality of achievement through human action. VISION has no boundaries and knows no limits. Our VISION is what we become in life." — **Tony Dungy**

Vision can be defined as an internalised mental picture of an ideal life—a preferable future. It is also defined as an internalised mental picture of your purpose. It is your ability to break down barriers, and in cases where the barriers cannot be broken, it is your ability to see beyond them. It is your ability to see that which cannot be perceived by the naked eyes. Vision is also the capacity to see that which others cannot see then plan and prepare for it.

Vision is a function of the heart while sight is a function of the eyes. Vision is far greater than sight. It is more powerful than sight. Let your vision, and not your sight, drive you daily; only then will you be able to live a truly fulfilling and purposeful life—one that no eyes (including yours) have been able to see or even perceive yet.

Helen Keller, one of the greatest motivational speakers and transformational leaders of our time, who was blind, dumb, and deaf from the tender age of 18 months (following an illness), was once asked in an interview what could be the worst tragedy that could ever happen to someone other than being born blind. Her response was simple, yet profound. Smiling, she wrote on a sheet of paper, "The only thing worse than being blind is having sight but no vision."

In effect, she demonstrated that having eyes wasn't indispensable for the fulfilment of her purpose; neither should being blind be an excuse to keep her from fulfilling her maximum potential. On the contrary, she travelled all over the world and impacted millions of lives through her inspirational speeches—even though she couldn't speak and was blind. She had an interpreter and could communicate by using a device and also by reading people's lips with her hands.

Here is someone we might think had limitations because she was blind and deaf, yet she understood the real power that determines how successful and fulfilled we become in life is our vision, our ideal, that internalized mental picture of the preferred life that we want for ourselves. She is a great example of someone who could have been labelled as disabled, yet she didn't let this impact her in any way. She spoke and transformed the lives of people like you and me who could see, speak, and hear. She was capable of transforming their lives, despite not being able to see, hear, or speak.

Hence, we should never settle for anything beneath our vision and our greatness. Your vision should be your ultimate focus and definition of your true self and purpose. Keep your eyes focused on your vision, the destination, and finale! You are destined for greatness and success.

As you read through this chapter, I dare you to be a visionary in the process! Arise... do not be afraid... Dare to break down the barriers of your thoughts and life that are holding you back and soar to greater heights. In cases where those barriers cannot be broken, dare to see beyond the mental barriers of your thoughts and physical barriers of your eyes... Dare to see beyond your current reality and challenges.

Dare to dream big, and remember this, no dream is unrealistic...it's only a matter of timing...be patient, though it tarries, it will surely come to pass. If you have conceived it, believed it, you must surely give birth to it. Believe in your vision, write it down on paper, make it clear and communicate it clearly... Let it stir up and ignite an unquenchable desire and passion within you, so you may be inspired and be able to inspire others to willingly join you in your cause.

"Throughout the centuries there were men who took first steps down new roads armed with nothing but their own vision. Their goals differed, but they all had this in common: that the step was first, the road new, the vision unborrowed, and the response

they received — hatred. The great creators — the thinkers, the artists, the scientists, the inventors — stood alone against the men of their time. Every great new thought was opposed. Every great new invention was denounced. The first motor was considered foolish. The airplane was considered impossible. The power loom was considered vicious. Anesthesia was considered sinful. But the men of unborrowed vision went ahead. They fought, they suffered and they paid. But they won."—Ayn Rand.

Dare to conceive a vision woman! The vision you conceive shall be great— because your seed shall be great! Dare to be a great woman... Dare to be you! Dare to be Unique and original and not a copy! Because you are an original, full of originality! No single child you ever bore in your womb and gave birth to has identical DNA. You are meticulously creative and constantly replenishing the earth with originals...one of a kind...

I hereby invite you to join me on this incredibly powerful and unforgettable journey to uncover and embrace your vision and make the most of the endless and astonishing opportunities awaiting you (such as those offered by this contemporary manuscript and inspirational authors), keeping in mind the indisputable fact that you are a victor and not a victim—born to stand out and soar like an eagle.

There's never been a more desperate and urgent need than now to understand what each one of us genuinely wants and needs; and pursue our greatest and most fulfilling heart's desires and life purpose. Before now, our world has never witnessed a generation of young, vibrant, and dynamic men and women who seem to be so distracted, lost, and without a clear sense of identity, vision, and purpose.

Awakening the Audacious and Visionary Child in You

If you could look back on your young and fearless self before society and parents started limiting you by telling you what is and is not possible to achieve, what would you see? What would you hear and above all who would you see?

I am privileged to have worked with thousands of women through my personal development and leadership training programs and teachings, and some of the most common statements or "excuses" I often hear when I run my cutting-edge "Develop Unwavering Confidence" and "Public Speaking" programs are: "I am shy, I have always been shy as a child," "I am an introvert and really don't like or feel comfortable expressing my thoughts, feelings, and opinions," "I am so afraid to express myself and often freeze and become speechless in the process." Maybe you are reading this now, and you could relate; as one or more of the above statements run through your mind too. Now I want you to pause for a moment and think about your early years of life (if you can remember) or the early years and even days of life of "any child" …

No child born to a woman and living is ever shy to express themselves and how they feel at any given moment in time. Have you ever seen a newborn baby who would be shy to scream and cry until their needs and demands are met? Do you remember when you needed that next meal (milk or breast milk), do you remember when you needed that next nappy change or was uncomfortable? Do you remember when you never wanted someone to invade your private space, look at you, touch you or carry you? Do you remember when someone took your toy or possession and you needed it back (irrespective of who they were or looked like)? Do you remember when you desired that toy in a shop, or even when it wasn't yours and belonged to another child? Were you truly ever shy or introverted? The simple answer is NO! NEVER! We learn to be shy; we learn to be an introvert – it is not in our nature to be shy and introverted, and it's never too late to unlearn these self-limiting attributes and qualities. It is my ultimate heart's desire that as I share my own journey with you and you read through the chapters of this book, your desire to awaken the incredible and audacious child in you is re-ignited and unstoppable!

As a child growing up in the beautiful nation of Cameroon, in the west of Africa, I was always a very confident little girl. Looking back on my childhood, I now realise that my dad played a very significant role in building my confidence... I think it's fair to say that I owe almost all of my confidence to my wonderful dad, which is one of the reasons why I wrote the book *A Father's Tender and Compassionate Love*. My mum was equally a very loving and caring mum, who expressed so much love and care towards me and my siblings as well.

My dad was an amazing father who taught me so much in life and empowered me to unlock my authentic identity, self-worth, and value and to never settle for any less. He profoundly believed in me, which translated into me believing in myself in return. Mum also profoundly believed in me, which further boosted my confidence.

At the tender age of seven, I was very confident and had a clear mental image (vision) of who I wanted to become and where I wanted to live when I grew up. I knew exactly (almost exactly) what I wanted in life. I wanted to become a medical doctor. Specifically, I wanted to become a gynaecologist. While growing up, there was a very successful and devoted gynaecologist in my neighbourhood who inspired me a great deal. I admired him so much that I also wanted to become a successful and outstanding gynaecologist. Furthermore, I wanted to study in Italy because said gynaecologist also studied in Italy. Despite knowing nothing about how I would get there or finance my studies, I was determined to study there and was very confident that, when that time came, I was actually going to study in Italy. My long-term goal was to eventually settle in the UK with my family because I did not want to settle in a non-English speaking country, since I am an Anglophone Cameroonian.

It was my greatest and somewhat only heart's desire to study for my doctorate degree in Italy ... and eventually settle in the United Kingdom. This was my dream, and I was confident I could achieve it...

In addition, I have always been a naturally curious child, intrigued and fascinated by the human body and how it functions to keep us alive and heal us when we get unwell. In fact, my dad used to call me (the smallest amongst my siblings then) his *pocket lawyer*... I guess I could only be a "pocket lawyer" then given how small I was.

Interestingly, my mum also called me her *"attorney general"*. You could instantly tell that this little child was no ordinary run-of-the-mill *"African child"* and there was something bigger in her. There was a seed of greatness in her and growing up in such a nurturing and loving environment greatly contributed to nourishing and nurturing that seed of greatness in me.

Nonetheless, as the youngest of five siblings and still attending primary school at the time, I had quite a journey to undertake and, to say the least, a great deal of "last born" hindrances to overcome. Did any of the above really matter to me or preoccupy me? Absolutely no! For example, the fact that by the time I got to university my beloved and hardworking parents must have spent a huge fortune on the education and welfare of my elder siblings didn't really make much difference to me and to my ability to dream beyond my wildest imaginations. What seemed to be the reality NEVER conditioned the magnitude of my dreams and heart's desires…

All I ever knew and thought of was becoming a gynaecologist and studying in Italy, with the intention of later settling in an English-speaking nation—specifically, England. In effect, I strongly believed that whatever I could conceive and believe in my mind I could undoubtedly achieve. I knew with great certainty that wherever there is a will there will definitely be a way—sooner or later.

As mentioned earlier, the only reason I chose Italy as my number 1 and only choice for university was that one of the most renowned gynaecologists in my city (who was my friend's dad and resided in my neighbourhood) earned his medical degree in Italy. I was greatly inspired by him and I immediately thought that in order to become an exceptional gynaecologist like he was, it was vital to study in Italy since that is where he studied! Never mind the fact that I was a seven-year-old girl! I was convinced that Italy was the best place to study medicine in the world—it was the real deal!

Consequently, I was determined to get and become the very best from Italy, and nothing else really mattered! Did I think of the cost implications? Absolutely no! Did I think of my elder siblings having to go to university before me, hence putting considerable burden on our parents' finances and resources? Absolutely no! Did I think about what my dad, mum, siblings, and even relatives thought about this? Absolutely no! Did I seek anyone's approval or opinion on this decision of mine? Absolutely no! All I knew was the fact that this was my dream and my dream alone, and I was responsible for making it become a reality... PERIOD. An audacious seven-year-old, right? No wonder Dad called me his "pocket lawyer" and Mum called me her "attorney general"!

My question to you is this: how many of us today have killed and buried that audacious and fearless little girl in us? How many of us have locked her within and thrown away the keys for fear of judgement, failure, rejection, pain, etc? How many of us no longer recognise her and constantly suppress her each time she is about to show up and express herself? How many of us have lost or silenced her forever, hoping we could pretend she never existed and she was an illusion? It is my heart's desire that as I share with you the incredibly courageous and fearless journey of this audacious little seven-year-old girl, it stirs up a new desire and unrest within your spirit to reconnect with the brave and fearless little girl in you – your inner child and most authentic and purest state of being and manifestation.

Now, let's fast-forward and see what became of that little confident seven-year-old girl who knew exactly what she wanted in life. Thirteen years have gone by so quickly, and I have just finished my A-level exams with an outstanding result. I am now ready to get into university but, most importantly, into a completely strange land and foreign nation where English wasn't even the first language—my Italy! Did everything go as smoothly as I had dreamt and envisaged? Not at all, but I will focus on the most gigantic mountain and barrier I have yet to encounter and overcome, hence highlighting my unshakable beliefs and confidence!

It was finally time for me to move to the capital of Cameroon, Yaoundé, to live with my eldest sister and study the Italian Language Course in the Italian Embassy, amongst other things. What a great six months I had studying the language weekly and getting acquainted with my new lifestyle. It was now four months into the course and everything was going so well. I was already fluent in Italian and, as always, I was one of the best students in my class! You see, I never get into anything I love with the intention of being anything less than the best! Neither do I go in with the intention of competing with others... I simply go in with one goal and one purpose only—to be and give my very best and only that! Most probably, others don't come in with this intention and that's why I almost always end up being the best 😊.

Visionary Woman

Life Tests are Designed to Stretch Us Beyond Our Comfort Zone and into Our Greatness

It was now time to write that famous and qualifying Italian Language Exam, which would determine and set apart those students who were ready and destined to fulfil their dreams and ambitions in Italy from the masses who had also been studying the language but would need to think of alternative options and dreams as their Italian dreams gradually faded away... Well, the confident Sylvia is never a stranger to exams and knew she was definitely destined for Italy to fulfil her long-term dream and vision of becoming a gynaecologist! But guess what? Oh well... The marking system that year had changed and a higher pass mark (well above average) was established in an attempt to allow fewer students from Cameroon to further their studies in Italy, I guess... It sounds like a pretty good excuse...

The results are finally out ... and guess what; no one in my class made it—not even me! We were told that apparently only one anglophone student in the entire nation made it beyond the higher qualifying threshold mark! Of note, this student lives in the French Cameroon region and also studied in the French education system... Notwithstanding, he is very intelligent and would never fail any exam! You may be asking, "But what has being anglophone or francophone got to do with this, Sylvia?"

Now, let me explain; the fact that Italian is a "Neo-Latin" language, and so too is French, makes it easier for French-speaking nationals or "francophones" to learn the language—hence the outstanding results from our francophone peers. On the contrary,

English is not a Neo-Latin language, which makes it a bit harder, yet possible, for English nationals or "anglophones" like my friends and me to study the language! I am by no means making an excuse for our unsuccessful results as such a barrier simply means that we have to work twice, thrice, or even 10x as hard … and why not?

I was thinking, *Is this the end of my Italian dream? Am I going to be the very one to sabotage my own dreams and ambitions?* I pondered. I am not the type to fail an exam for whatever reason; I am not the type to easily give up in the face of a "failure" or "mountain". My sister was heartbroken and disappointed to see my 13-year dream suddenly come to an end or so she thought… *I am never going to deliver a message of failure to my dad or mum. I have never been a failure and I am not ready to become one now.* I thought. They had never known me to ever fail an exam that was based on merit, hard work, intelligence, you name it … and I was not ready to introduce this new concept to them just yet! I was thinking, *Dad has made a huge sacrifice to ensure I finally go and further my studies in Italy, and I am not ready just yet to be the one to blow all of this up—No Way!*

Vision Empowers Us with Unwavering Confidence and Courage

I was about to carry out one of the most unrealistic and courageous acts that would change the life course for many anglophone Cameroonians including me! I told my sister I was going to call the ambassador's home and speak with him. Of note, I was not asking for her consent; neither was I asking for her opinion on this. I was simply giving her notice, and being polite of course, since I was to use her landline to make the call!

I vividly remember picking up the telephone directory and searching for the Italian ambassador to Cameroon's residential telephone number, which I got! My rationale for not even attempting to call the Italian Embassy was to bypass the many obstacles and barriers I would have encountered to get to him. Calling the embassy would mean having to go through the secretary, cultural attaché', and many more people before getting to him (if at all I was fortunate enough to get to him), something I had no intention of doing!

I then embarked on my next phase—CALLING THE AMBASSADOR! I remember picking up the phone and confidently dialling the ambassador's number! How could I ever forget this very crucial and decisive moment? I was sitting there relaxed and ready to share my concerns as the phone rang... Then, suddenly, "Hello," a lady's voice echoed from the other end of the phone.

"Hello," I responded.

Behold, it was the ambassador's wife and this was my moment! I introduced myself to her in Italian, trying my best to sound mature. We engaged in a good six or seven-minute conversation, maybe even longer in "undiluted" Italian. She was amazed by my fluent Italian and remarked, "But you speak Italian very well, how come you did not pass the exam?" This was my final chance to resolve the crisis we were faced with or regret my entire life!

I then explained in fluent Italian how the change in the scoring system had left many anglophones, including me, very disadvantaged, despite knowing and speaking the language very well. I also told her that I was amongst the best students in my class but none of us made it! I made her understand that the purpose of my call was to request another chance for us all from her husband, the ambassador; another test, in whatever format they desired, including an oral test where we would be able to prove how fluent we were in Italian!

She was absolutely lovely and very empathetic and compassionate too! She immediately requested that I write a letter expressing my concerns and a proposal, addressing it to the ambassador, and taking—it personally to the embassy—where the ambassador would be expecting it. I then expressed my heartfelt gratitude to her and wished her a good night.

Now I was super excited and immediately reached for the phone again to call my other friends (who were also amongst the best in my class) and arrange a meeting the next day! I also called our Italian teacher, Sister Paula, who absolutely loved us and was very disappointed with the outcome of the exam results; remember, we were her brightest students but didn't make it! I asked if she could endorse a letter written by my friends and me (we were four in number), which she happily and instantly agreed to! Besides, she requested that we meet with her once we had drafted the letter. We wasted no time in getting this done the next day and going over to see her with the draft. She read it, was impressed, and endorsed it, backing it up with a statement confirming that we were the very best of her class and some of the best students she had ever worked with. How I wish I had kept a copy of this letter!

Finally, it was time to take the weighty letter to the embassy and deliver it as requested. Within a week of handing in that powerful letter, an official communication was made over the radio calling all Cameroonian anglophones from the entire nation who took the exam in different regions of the country that year but didn't succeed (even though they scored above average) for a second chance! Yes, a second chance! An oral exam! This had never happened in the country's history! Yet, that isolated and unrealistic, courageous, and purpose-driven phone call changed the nation's history forever! Everyone involved from the entire nation was summoned to the Italian Embassy in the nation's capital for the first Italian oral exam ever! This day forever changed the life course of many ... Many who were once declined were now accepted and set to travel to Italy to fulfil their ambitions and dreams, including me of course. Except for my three friends and me, none of them knew what actually happened behind the scenes that led to this fateful day that changed their lives forever!

Never change your vision, lose confidence in yourself, or lower the bar because of life circumstances, as there will be many in your lifetime. On the contrary, believe in yourself, re-strategize, and stay focused on your dreams and vision. The only real limitation to what we can achieve or become is our mind, in the beliefs we cultivate and hold about ourselves. If only you and I believe, we would be able to remove the endless and seemingly insurmountable mountains that get in our way of success and greatness.

Dr Sylvia Forchap-Likambi et al

Vision Ignites an Unquenchable Drive, Passion, and an Unwavering Conviction to Succeed.

As a very inquisitive and curious child who was always asking questions about almost everything and anything, most of which ended up without satisfactory answers, I immediately understood that I had a lot of work to do in order to satisfy my curiosity and insatiable quest for knowledge and also get more compelling answers to my questions. I needed to research more, learn more, and discover more...

This was my inspiration and drive for getting into the pharmaceutical field and, eventually, into medical research. With an in-depth knowledge of drugs, medical research would enable me to identify new prognostic and diagnostic tools/factors.

I then went on to earn my PhD in Italy (with a special focus on leukaemia, a type of blood cancer), during which time I also studied in Sydney, Australia, as part of my PhD program. At the end of my PhD, I then worked in Italy for a year, after which I was ready to move on and fulfil my childhood dream of settling in the UK. This meant I only applied for jobs in the UK and was successfully offered two different jobs in two different hospitals and cities.

To me, it didn't matter where I came from or what skin tone and gender I had. Of note, when I applied for these jobs, no one knew me in these hospitals, nor did I know anyone. I also applied as a Cameroonian citizen, which meant that if I was offered any of the jobs, I would need to get a working permit and visa to be able to migrate to the UK and take up the position.

Once I was offered the jobs and made my decision about which one to accept, I then had to apply for a working visa from the British Embassy in Rome, Italy. As part of the application process, a series of documents was required, which included a working permit issued by my new British employer and a letter explaining why an African (a non-European citizen) was offered the role when there are a lot of British and European citizens with similar qualifications and experiences. In a nutshell, they wanted to know whether the employers had considered and exhausted all their options of offering the job to their British and neighbouring European citizens without success before finally offering the opportunity to an African (me in this case)! In response to this requisite, I received the letter and my work permit from my new British employer to support my application. In this letter it was emphasised that amongst all of the candidates interviewed (I think 38 or so, I can't quite remember the exact number now) for the position, I was the best candidate with the right set of skills, qualities, expertise, and experiences that best met the specifications they needed for the job. Consequently, it was never about race, nationality, background, and gender but about the unique traits and qualities of the ideal candidate, which I fully met.

So, why am I sharing this with you? How relevant is it? My reason is simple and straightforward. When you know who you are (which is defined by your vision and purpose), you stand tall; you are confident; you believe in yourself whether others believe in you or not; you set the example; you set the pace because you so much believe in yourself; you walk confidently and people notice that there is something unique about you and the way you present yourself and they are attracted to you, irrespective of your race, gender, and background. Some may even ask, "What is it about this woman?" "What is it about this man?" and they eventually start to believe in you because you demonstrate this trait consistently in everything you do. Hence, knowing who you are and having a clear vision for your life gives you unwavering confidence that makes you courageous and fearless and opens up endless doors and opportunities for you.

Finding Your Vision

It's very obvious that wherever you are on the planet right now and reading this book, you are actually in the present. But after this day what next? After the next day what next? Where is your journey leading you to? Where are you going? What is your destination? What is the great plan? Examine these questions in greater depth. Visualise your future... What does it look like? How does it feel? Where do you want to be or would rather be to be genuinely happy, at peace, and fulfilled?

If success was guaranteed for everything you do and failure is never an option, what will you be spending your time and days doing? If you never had to work for a wage or to meet your personal and financial needs, because you were the wealthiest woman in the universe, where would you rather be or live and what would you do while in this ideal destination? It's simply not enough to get to where you want to or live in your dream home. For example, so many people go to university but go for different reasons. Some are teachers, some are professors, some are students, some are cleaners, some are trainees, etc. So, what will you do when you get to that final destination? Why are you going there and not somewhere else? Why would you have this vision and not another? All of the above are critical questions to be addressed which will take you closer to your life purpose.

Finally, once you have arrived at your dream destination, you know why you're there, and you're now working towards fulfilling the latter. A final and conclusive question you must ask and seek to genuinely respond to is this… How does it feel?

How will you feel when you finally get to that final destination of your journey and you are now doing all the things you went there to accomplish? What does finishing the journey mean to you? What's the ultimate price that awaits you at the end of this journey? What does success mean to you and feel like? If your answers to this last question (which is all about the way you feel) create fulfillment, satisfaction, inner peace, and that "Wow" effect, then this is really where you were born to be and what you were born to accomplish—your purpose! If your responses are like, "I'm going to feel really great; I'm going to feel powerful and amazing; I'm going to feel fulfilled; I am going to feel accomplished and successful; I am going to feel incredibly awesome," then go for it! This is actually who you were born to be and in becoming that person, you have not only found your authentic identity, but you have also fulfilled your ultimate purpose of living.

In addition, this is where you were born and destined to be and what you were born to be doing when you get to that destination.

As a result, by the time you eventually exit this planet, you will be holding nothing back and will leave a lasting legacy behind. In other words, you must have fulfilled your maximum potential, benefited your children, your generation, humanity, and left a legacy.

Success is not necessarily about amassing riches and all of the material stuff around us... We know of so many whom society has defined as successful people, who have unfortunately felt empty, void, worthless, and eventually taken away their own lives by committing suicide. It is therefore very evident that success is not about amassing riches, but rather, it is about knowing who you are – your purpose – and living a fulfilling and purposeful life.

As I come to the end of this chapter, I would urge you to start working on your unique journey to uncovering your vision and life purpose – if you haven't done so yet, and set the necessary goals to fulfil your vision and make it a tangible reality. You are a visionary, born and designed for greatness! Go now and live a life of authenticity, greatness, and purpose.

Chapter Two

WE ARE GOD'S HANDIWORK

By Dr Anikpe Oyedeji

Appreciation

I approached Dr Sylvia in February to assist me in writing a book on my heart, "Behold He Comes," to celebrate my golden jubilee. I was pleasantly surprised when she, in the course of our conversation, told me she perceived I had something to say on her project on a Visionary and Purposeful Woman. Thank you for the opportunity to share and reflect on my journey so far in life. I hope to bring readers over the next few pages into what has motivated me, inspired me, and brought me this far in life (and love)! I would certainly never have considered myself or my life story as particularly visionary or interesting enough to share. I also extend my thanks to all visionary and purposeful readers who pick this up to read my words. Thank you!

Biodata

Dr Anikphe Oyedeji currently lives in northwest England and works part-time in North Wales as a Consultant Physician at the NHS. She has been married for 20 years to Dr Ade, an Ordained

Minister of the Gospel of Christ. Their purpose is to build the Body of Christ through apostolic teaching into fullness of maturity in Christ so the church is ready to welcome the return of Jesus Christ as King into the next age, his millennial reign. Together for 12 years, they have planted a local church in Ellesmere Port and ran the New Creation Centre, a community outreach project. She is a mother of four amazing children whom God has given her the privilege to develop as His gifts to the world. For the past 12 years, she has also co-owned a franchise care-at-home business. Life has been full to the brim. It's been a tough act, juggling so many balls and trying not to drop many, but His grace has been more than sufficient. Anikphe readily admits that it is a balancing act living out these various roles as co-labourer of Christ, career woman, mother, home-builder, and business owner while holding on to one of her main aims in life, which is to do all things with excellence and to the glory of God. In her contribution to this book, she shares her life-building story and her life journey so far, including low points and high points. She especially shares her story from the angle of how the promises of God and the Word of His Grace have been supernaturally sufficient. Her story lets us into God's handiwork in building her into the visionary and purposeful woman that we see today for His glory. But He is not done yet; her aim is to become God's fully mature and developed masterpiece.

What I have discovered as a challenge many women face is how to resolve our conflicts between where you are and where you would like to be; conflict between what you dreamt to be and where you are at presently and the roles that society thrusts upon you. At other times, the conflict is in our hearts – where our voice and dream are silenced, or we are being told our thoughts do not matter. Be it by fathers or husbands or other significant men, which distract you from your purpose. These are struggles many women face. The Lord knows I have struggled in these areas too.

In the first fifty years of my life, I have learned some truths about life that have helped me negotiate these landmines and get to a place where I am moving more into my ministry—which I will describe as a refocusing ministry. As a woman, my most important lesson so far is to remain connected to God and to understand what He is doing at each time, not just in me but in relation to the larger picture of God's household economy. Only then have I become more effective. In Christ, and as a Woman today, I am finally coming to a place where I am learning to own my spaces in life, to enjoy every bit of my way through them, and, most importantly, to live the "good life" to its fullest every day.

WORDS MATTER

As a young woman in my late teens and early 20s, I found I learned a lot and got answers to my questions on life from listening to songs, scriptures, and stories. Words from certain songs, scriptures, and stories have conveyed exceedingly great and precious promises from God to me. They have influenced my decision-making and my choices. Many of these words have reverberated in the core of my being, and have helped me remain intentional in my enjoyment of life. I believe strongly that words carry life and that my spoken words have shaped my past and present. Words, I have found, have the power to bring themselves to pass. The words I speak today over my life, my home, my marriage, my children, my career, my finances, and my future carry within themselves the power of life and death.

Conversely, I have learned that words can be poisonous and that certain words, contrary to God's plan as revealed in his Word, must not be allowed into my heart. It is in my power to choose and control which words to allow into my heart, or words I speak with my mouth. Negative words I find to be like barometers that express our thoughts and could potentially influence the course of life adversely if not redirected speedily.

My dad used to say, "Words are like eggs, once you release them in speech, they are broken and can never be put back together again." He taught us as his children to be careful about what we said with our tongues. He would often say, "Your tongue and the power of speech that you have is what distinguishes you as a human being, so be careful what you say." One powerful practical habit that has helped me immensely in the past 15 years is to play the audio bible in my home and car 24/7. His words wash me clean and I often hear a word in season that changes everything.

DEVELOPING A CHRIST MINDSET

I have learned progressively to bring my desires to God again and again in order to be purified. My own words to God, when spoken over my life, or when voiced out in prayer, especially as I express myself through songs and in the Spirit, have given my heart's desires many chances to be purified and exchanged for His higher ones for me. I have learned that for me, success in life is about receiving God's help so that in incremental steps I can say he has helped me do what he has required of me. And I do my best to think thoughts that are in line with these words which I believe and hold on to as true. I continually bring my speaking, even in jest, to be consistent and in line with these beliefs in my heart. The following scriptures are the bedrock of my mindset. They speak of vision and how our vision is enfolded in God and how we should rest in him and trust in him.

- "God works in us both to will and do of his good pleasure" Philippians 2.13

- "For we are God's [own] handiwork (His workmanship), recreated in Christ Jesus, [born anew] that we may do those good works which God predestined (planned beforehand) for us [taking paths which He prepared ahead of time], that we should walk in them [living the good life which He prearranged and made ready for us to live]" Ephesians 2:10 AMPC

- "Martha, Martha, thou art careful and troubled about many things: but *one thing is needful*: and Mary hath chosen that good part, which shall not be taken away from her."

- Luke 10:41-42 KJV

These scriptures, and many others, have helped me rest in my position in Christ, receive strength, and have courage. These words help me avoid the stress and strain of bearing the responsibility of living purposefully in my frail human strength and human wisdom.

Dear Reader, you too have a High Purpose in your Maker. He has a plan for your life. His foremost desire for each one of us is to fulfil His purpose. He wants you and I, all of us, to live His best life for us, to enjoy the good life, and to have great success in all we do.

A Christ-like mindset has guided me, shaped my life journey, and given me the power of focus on my set goals, and to pursue them in order to press and reach and to attain my dreams despite adversities. I have a mindset in me that my dreams are in line with my heart's desires, and that my heart's desires are God-inspired.

THE POWER OF DREAMS

Childhood:

I have learned that my life today is the summation of dreams I dreamt in my yesterdays. I cast my mind back and remember growing up in Ibadan, Oyo State in the south-western region of Nigeria. As a little girl, I first discovered the world around me through books and stories I read. Ibadan was described to me by J.P. Clark, in one poem I learnt in 1983, as the city "scattered among seven hills" with "glistening brown roofs in the sun."

Dreaming Big

I remember my dreams as a young girl were of travelling far away to America, of being "the best" and of "making discoveries." Our bookshelves were filled with books bought by my mother and I would often escape from house chores to secret hideouts in our family home where no one expected me to be in order to feast on stories from faraway places. I dreamt of greatness as I got myself lost in reading story books. I strived to excel in my schoolwork and found that doing well in school got me positive attention from my parents and their friends. I enjoyed the positive feelings and attention, so I learned more and tried even harder to do even better next time. I first dreamt of becoming a doctor at age 8 after a visit to the local clinic.

Pursuing my Dreams through Education

My parents and grandparents never allowed me to forget my dream of becoming a doctor. I was reminded again and again as I grew up, that "when I grow up, I want to be a doctor!" My dreams and mindset led me to work hard and excel in school. I entered medical school easily enough and graduated from University of Ibadan Medical School in 1994, with a distinction at the young age of 22 years. After working for a year as a House Officer in Paediatrics and Obstetrics and Gynaecology at University College Hospital Ibadan, I decided to leave Nigeria to pursue the next step in my dreams of excelling and greatness by continuing my house jobs in Surgery and Medicine at Korle-Bu Teaching hospital in Accra Ghana, which was affiliated with the University of Ghana for another one year to escape the political instability mirrored by incessant strikes in Nigerian universities, hospitals, and what I perceived as certain mediocrity lurking around the corner for me.

Upon the completion of my internship in Accra in 1996, I juggled three jobs to raise and save enough money to enable me to pay for travel to pursue my curiosity further, first by travelling to London to enrol in a master's degree in Immunology at Imperial College in October 1996. I pushed through financial difficulties and debt as an overseas student in a London University, while simultaneously obtaining a Certificate in Ministry from Kingsway International School of Ministry in London and studying to pass my Professional Linguistic Assessment Board (PLAB) examinations so I could practise as a doctor in U.K., which I did in April 1997. Subsequently, in addition to getting some financial aid and scholarships, I put a pause on my master's studies for six months after passing so I could work as a junior doctor in London hospitals and save money to clear my debts. Then I went back as soon as I could to continue studying during the week while still working on the weekends and some night shifts on weekdays to pay off my schooling debts. I eventually graduated in 1998 with another distinction. My next immediate desire was to relocate to accomplish an even bigger dream in my heart of obtaining a US green card and winning a Nobel Prize through my research.

More Travelling and More Growing Up

These goals led me to seize an opportunity to obtain a US green card "without a job offer" in an advert I noticed in the British Medical Journal one day. My desires paved the way and got me to the USA in 1998, with plenty of hope. I attempted to begin my residency program in Internal Medicine in October 1998 at the University of Connecticut, but at that point, life became more complicated as I made space in my life to include men, relationships, and marriage. Coupled with increasing distances from established support networks like my nuclear family and my local church, I was introduced to other dimensions of life that included delays, disappointment, and apparent defeat and failure. My next three years between 1998 and 2001 taught me how to deal with some of the other Ds of life: Distractions, denials, delays, disappointment, disease, death…

EARLY LESSONS LEARNED

Delay is not Denial

It was in 2001 when I first learned a truth that holds constant: "My Golgotha hill actually really holds keys to my resurrected life and dream. My greatest pains in life I have learnt are opportunities for me to press on into God's best for me." ----------------

I learned that "delay is not denial," "beyond every disappointment and cloud in life is a silver lining," and "the sun does come out at the end of every heavy storm and after the rain is a rainbow as surely as day follows night." I also learned that no weapon formed against me can prosper and that even if I seem to be down, no apparent defeat in my life is ever permanent, and that living life is not over until God says it is over. I learned to hold on to God's promises and that His faithfulness is forevermore. I learned that even in the places of greatest challenge and apparent defeat in my life, or even the "death of a dream" for that matter, that this place also holds opportunity for me through the power of resurrection for greatness and glory.

In addition, I've learned that life unfolds itself in phases. Each phase can be conceptualised as coinciding with a season. My life experiences can be likened to Summer, Autumn, Winter, and Spring. Just like the seasons of life require different actions from a farmer, so do our lives. However, our lives unfold concurrent seasons in different areas and a trick I have learned works well is to keep a close watch during each season on what is the one needful thing I must be doing continually.

How to Cause Life to Spring Forth from Dream-Ashes

For me, my *"one thing needful"* has been sitting with the Master with the attitude of a big DONE IN CHRIST. Jesus Christ has won the victory for me already. He has called me to learn Christ and to learn how to enforce the victory that is already mine in Christ. I must learn to SIT to enjoy what Christ has done for me. I must sow God's word into the various areas of my life intentionally. I have learned to repose on His promises and to lay down the burden of my anxieties and my fears. I have learned to rest in and repose in utter trust, letting him bear the responsibility of fulfilling His Words to me and to cease carrying the weight of it all myself. That is the way I have found that I can continually bring life out of ashes so I can eventually reap a bountiful harvest of righteousness, peace and joy no matter the circumstances life presents me.

Let me explain what I mean…

In the late 1990s, while studying and growing up, I travelled a lot and kept moving farther and farther away from home in search of my "greener pastures." I moved from Ibadan, near my parents and family, to moving to live and practise farther away; first in Accra, Ghana, then to London, England, then followed by moving through various states in the USA from Hartford, Connecticut to Cleveland, Ohio and Silver Spring, Maryland to practise medicine, but I had to wait for my immigration papers to be granted before I could start. Ultimately, not only did I not get my green card as expected, I was jilted in a "failed courtship" and found myself having to leave the United States quickly to escape becoming an undocumented immigrant. It was a very trying and disorienting season in my life. When I eventually landed on my feet, I found myself back in Coventry, United Kingdom. The weights of disappointment and even depression left me feeling that pursuing my dreams had led me nowhere during that two-year period!

Nonetheless, God worked it out for me and within another one year I turned a bend that got me my desired US green card and the same job that came back even better which then took me back to Hartford, CT again! So, from age 24 to 29, it was like my life did a full circle. You can only imagine what a roller-coaster such momentous life events had on me and the negative impact of these upheavals on my younger self during those migratory years.

But to God be the glory, and I instead came out on the other end wiser, more resilient, and stronger. I look back on these years with great thanksgiving. For me, those 5-6 years, despite the great challenges they presented, laid great foundational character stones in my life and character.

Alone? Crushed, yet not forsaken.

And during much of these times I was "alone."

Far from home, telephone technology in 1996 was not as good as it is today. Internet technology was in its infancy, as were emails. There was no social media. My first mobile phone was in 2001, and I relied on BT coin boxes and very expensive phone cards to call family and friends back in Nigeria. There were occasional handwritten letters posted through snail mail. I remember during that period red double-decker buses had BT adverts emblazoned on them stating "It is good to talk." Another ad on telly raised the question, "Good for who?" And then my friends and I would chuckle and say "Good for the business people" who made heaps of money off us! For most of that time, I was under immense financial pressure and had loads of exams to pass. In that period, I found that my greatest anchor was my faith evident by finding a Bible-based church and believers to fellowship. In the local church, I got my hands stuck on the plough as a labourer in the Lord's harvest field. I have found a big safety, a source of protection and strength in being under a Pastoral covering. Serving in the body of Christ also gives me a place for feeding necessary for normal healthy growth in my personal walk with God and relationship with Christ.

However, more importantly, I have been reading my Bible personally, developing the habit of my regular quiet times with the Lord, and of memorising scriptures actively by writing them out on index cards and muttering them, thereby putting them on my lips and speaking them over various situations that I have faced. These have been great sources of strength for my soul. The fruits of peace in my heart that these times have borne in my life have been tremendous.

These words for me have often been the difference between life and death. Giving up or pressing through. Failing or succeeding. These words have calmed my heart when anxious, driven out my fears and borne fruits of peace in my heart in the midst of storms. Another good Word for me has been Proverbs 3:5-6, and I find myself coming back to it again and again. It says "Lean on, trust in, and be confident in the Lord with all your heart and mind and do not rely on your own insight or understanding. In all your ways know, recognize, and acknowledge Him, and He will direct and make straight and plain your paths." Proverbs 3:5 -6 AMPC

LIVING MY DREAM

A Blossoming Medical Career

During my second stint in the United Kingdom between 1999 and June 2001, I was finally able to pass my Membership of the Royal College of Physicians Part I and 2 examinations. I completed my general medical training as well and had the opportunity to progress into higher specialty training in the UK, but my heart was still set on the United States, and I chose to go back to my original residency program. I reapplied and got accepted for June 2001. Once I settled into my internal medicine residency program in the University of Connecticut, I progressed quickly, was fast-tracked after only six months into my second year, completed that and progressed into a fellowship in Nephrology at the University of Pennsylvania, followed by subspecialty training in Transplant Nephrology. So by 2007, I was a Board Certified Internist, a Board Certified Nephrologist, and a

Dr Sylvia Forchap-Likambi et al

UNOS Certified Transplant Physician in the United States. My interest in Academic Medicine and Research had also materialised and I had my own funding from the NIH (National Institutes of Health) for my work in translational research with interest in preventing autoimmune diseases. I was writing papers and publishing in top journals and as my Chief Resident had put it "the world was my oyster," it was time to get a lovely job in a University on an academic track and live my dream.

Choosing a Life Partner

However, God had a plan. On my return to the United Kingdom in September 1999, I was found as a wife! A classmate from my school days in Ibadan had moved to London and came looking for me. He proposed to me and I accepted his proposal, but made it known to him that my heart was set on returning to the United States. So I returned to the United States and he remained in the United Kingdom.

Waiting till I had my education behind me and I was solidly on a career path was a double-edged sword. For my first 30 years of life, I had attained a high sense of fulfilment and accomplished great achievements of my vision and early dreams for my life through single-minded pursuit, but this also meant that when the pull of family commitments came it was very difficult for me to deal with the initially strong pull of a successful career versus the weaker pull of family life. It has taken me the past 15 years to understand the sacrifices women often have to make to raise a strong family and well-balanced and adjusted children that fully fulfil their destinies in society. Children need their mothers present. Until 2006, I had never had to make any compromises for a husband or family to have what I wanted or to pursue my own dreams!

RESOLVING MY CONFLICTS

Enlarging My Dream into God's Plan

The minute I married, new and strong desires were awakened within me, and these newly aroused desires for my family in God's plan conflicted with my quest for fame and success in my medical career. After a few years, we found ourselves in huge debt running two homes on two continents, spending a lot of money on transatlantic flights, visiting each other every few weeks, and suffering from expensive phone bills. We felt these things were extremely important to keep connected and the multiple holidays and "repeated honeymoons" were very enjoyable.

After six years of living that way with a 4-year-old daughter, I found I had to make a choice of either continuing my career trajectory in the United States while my husband and daughter took a back seat in my life by remaining in the United Kingdom and Nigeria (where I had sent my daughter to live with my brother when my live-in nanny walked out from the job). Or I had to return to England and allow a compromise on living my dream career. I had to face the unattractive prospect of building a new career in England with my main focus changing to building a home. The Bible says a wise woman builds her home in Proverbs 14:1, and several other scriptures pointed out that all roads were leading me back to England.

Dr Sylvia Forchap-Likambi et al

Returning to join my husband in his own endeavours in England was the top choice for several reasons - practical, financial, spiritual, and common sense. The Bible also counselled me to be secondarily adapted to my husband (1 Peter 3:1-7 and Ephesians 5:21- 33). My pastor in the US also told me that I needed to return to England to start my married life properly so my husband and I could pull together as a unit.

Despite the strong conviction about my return to the UK as the right decision, I battled with discontent and mourned a loss of direction for the next several years of my life. I did not find it as easy as many women do to make home-building and children my main focus. For many years I longed to have my career in the USA back.

But I have finally let go of that dream. In 2021, I allowed it to become ashes in order to embrace the next level God had planned for me. Even though my mind knew that it was the right choice to return to the UK for the third time, it was a difficult one for my soul, and for a long time I struggled with feelings that held me back. Even with God's help, I still found it very difficult until I let go of those American dreams and let them die and turn to ash after 13 years! I can finally relate with what many women mean when they mourn the loss of their careers because of starting families. As women, we really need God's grace to open our eyes to see His plan and to release us into His true purpose for us in marriage, as wives and as mothers.

PRESSING HIGHER

Since my return to the United Kingdom, we have been blessed with three more children. My husband's interests have led us into ministry work proclaiming the gospel of Christ. We planted a church in Cheshire, Northwest England, ran a community centre as an outreach into our local community, and owned a care-at-home care business. In between all that, I squeezed some medical work whenever I could. I found myself operating far outside my natural gifts and strengths. Being a doctor is the easy bit, yet it's the bit I am now called to do least!

Succeeding at all of the other things has required supernatural ability beyond myself and leaving my safe space! For excelling at being a wife, building a home, and raising children, I have had to dig deep inside and develop new skill-sets. To function as an entrepreneur, wife, mother, and home-builder, I have had to embrace sacrifice and serving in the process, and have needed plenty of wisdom and grace available from God to help me every day.

I am learning more and more to go to God in prayer again and again, and to ask for help with my weaknesses. I have needed so much of His grace, to see life from His perspective, and so much of His grace helped make me into the best me I can be; as a helper to my Life Partner, in home-building, ministry work, and raising four children into Christ's full plan and destiny in God. Every day I am still pressing higher into God's destiny and plan for me, both as an individual and in the context of my other roles.

The world's creation is groaning because it needs each woman fully mature, rising up in assurance of God's plan for her life, and her role in his Household. Women must be filled to express Christ fully for God's glory. We must embrace the inevitable change during various seasons of our life's journey. The foundation for all of these is knowing Jesus and building a personal relationship with him as the way to receive wisdom and grace to navigate through our journey of life. We need an abundance of grace, and all his gifts of righteousness. If we invest in this relationship, we will walk on His platforms of glory and we will reign in this life in Christ Jesus.

CHAPTER THREE

ALL IN THE NAME

By Dr Elizabeth Fon

BIODATA:

Born on August 28, 1958, as the first born of 10 children to a primary school teacher and his home-maker wife in the northwest region of Cameroon.

In form 3 while in the St Bede's secondary school, she plucked up the courage to do physics since it was more or less a confirmed fact at the time that girls had to do domestic science to become good housewives while the boys did physics and mathematics to become engineers and doctors. Leadership came knocking early in her life when in form 4, she was appointed the lone Senior Prefect (SP) for boys and girls in a mixed college, most of whom were boys. The boys felt slighted and started planning a strike action. However, in a few short weeks, she convinced the boys that she needed them as her teammates and they worked with her to the end of form five without any conflicts.

She has always done things that she was told only boys should do. That paved the way for her to develop a different mindset on how to interact and work with males in leadership roles because some years out of medical school, she had to head an all-male theatre team in the Bonassama District hospital in Douala.

As the first female DMO (District Medical Officer) of the Bonassama/Djebale/Cap Cameroon Health District, she had to lead male colleagues across the Atlantic high sea to control health epidemics on the islands.

All of the above constituted adequate preparation for her when she was appointed the Littoral TB/HIV control program chief, coordinating the activities of 200 nurses/doctors/support staff in 39 treatment centers where about 6,000 TB/HIV patients receive healthcare a year. That gave birth to the TESHO-Team Spirit Holistic program with a mission to teach life skills for stress reduction in Work/Life Balance. She has co-authored two books with her husband; "A Great Husband for a Great Wife" published in 2014 and "RECONCILE? NO WAY!" to be released soon.

Born in a remote village, through the grace of God, she has evolved into a female leader who listens to people and meets their needs so they can experience their best life ever, a job that is more rewarding than silver and gold.

A BABY IS BORN

When a baby is born, the parents go through a transformation. Their chests heave with emotions of awe, pride and gratitude for this baby with a wrinkly face. In that split instance, they fall head over heels in love with that small bundle of joy. Then they immediately start having great dreams for their baby. It doesn't matter if they are poor or rich, literate or illiterate, handsome or plain, having a baby marks a new page in the parents' lives, giving them the possibility to dream of a lofty future for their baby with them occupying a prominent place in that future. That happened to my primary school teacher dad and my homemaker/farmer mom. Then came the naming ceremony. The naming ceremony in our Meta tradition is a big deal because we believe that the name a baby is given will determine how the baby turns out in life because they will pick up many of the characteristics of the person whose name they are given.

When I was born on the 28th of August, 1958, in Cameroon, my parents were as overjoyed as any other couple. Being the first child, my father had the honour of naming me. I am sure he had spent entire nights calculating how he was going to name his first child. Now, this is how I came to be named; my dad was so smitten by the young Queen of England that he promptly named me Elizabeth. Then he added his mother's name to make it a solid combination. I was named Elizabeth Ijang.

Growing up was another adventure for me. I was raised by my Aunty and her husband, whom I will call Aunty and Uncle for purposes of comprehension because they were my mother and father in every sense of the word. They had lost all their three children and my dad gave me to them to raise as theirs from the age of about two years. The love they showered on me left no room for me to desire a life with my biological parents. It was later on in primary school that I knew about my biological parents. I was glad to have two sets of parents – my REAL mom and dad and my biological parents. I spent time with both sets of parents.

My two sets of parents chose love and a strict up-bringing as the only options for me. I had a double portion of the core values that a child needs to grow up into a balanced adult in sub-Saharan Africa.

USING THE POWER IN A NAME

From when I could recognize my environment and understand spoken language, my parents reminded me almost daily about the significance of my names. Whenever I would try to wriggle out of doing some difficult chores, they knew exactly how to get me to do them. It was all in the name. My mother would put on this act, "Queen Elizabeth, my one and only mother-in-law. Please can you go fetch some wood for your daughter-in-law who loves you so much"? How can a little girl resist such treatment? This went from doing chores, reading hard to pass exams, behaving well and I am sure I would have climbed Mount Cameroon backwards if they had asked me. It was all linked to the power in a name. My parents did not have much in the way of financial and material gifts for us and their children but each of their 10 children had a special name and a special place in their hearts. It was linked to the names they had given us and the words they used to build us up. With their words, we fabricated our own toys from the materials we found in our environment. Without any cajoling, we would gladly read using the light from a kerosene lamp or the flickering light from the fire. Reading under those "difficult conditions", we were able to pass our exams with flying colours. I say "difficult conditions" in quotes because we did not see our conditions as difficult. When we got home with good report cards, our parents would offer us more uplifting words than we knew what to do with.

There was a flip side to my name though. Whenever I heard my father call me Ijang or Elizabeth without adding the "my mother" or the "Queen," I knew I was in trouble. I would start building up excuses in my mind. If I did something wrong, my parents did not need to thrash me. All they needed to do was give me "that look" accompanied with a sharp Ijang or Elizabeth. I say "that look" in quotes because it was a look that packed in tons of disappointment, sorrow, sadness, and pity for the Queen that I wasn't. A look that made me cry inside with shame for letting down the Queen that I was supposed to be. The Queen of England surely did not know about the existence of a small girl in the forest of Africa, but her name was enough to mold that girl into the woman that she is today.

GOING OUT INTO THE WORLD

At the age of 11, I left the protection and comfort of our home and ventured into the world. I went to boarding school in St Bede's College in northwest Cameroon. Maybe other children upon leaving their parents had cried but I was kind of excited to go discover a new environment. At home, I used to share a bed with my sisters. The bed was a hard plank on which a mat was thrown. My junior sisters would bring sand into bed with them (we all ran around barefooted so climbing into bed with sand was kind of natural for the younger ones). On some nights, they would do "water works" in bed... I am sure you get my drift. I would be jolted awake as I turned and came into contact with the chilly urine. Today, we are told that a hard surface is good for the back and that sand can be the equivalent of acupuncture.

The St Bedes Reverend sisters insisted that every parent who wanted their child to study in St Bedes had to buy everything on the prospectus. Suddenly, I became the proud owner of my own grass mattress, a box containing bedsheets, plates, a cup, cutlery and a good number of dresses. For a girl like me who could count all she had ever owned on less than the fingers on one hand, I saw myself as super rich when I entered secondary school. That was the mindset of abundance and gratitude that set me firmly on the path of studies. I was so eager to study that I was made the library caretaker to arrange the books and record the names of all who borrowed books to read. I simply devoured all the books in the library. I could be in St Bede's but be dancing in Paris, cruising on the Caribbean Sea or building an igloo in Greenland. That was the power in reading books for a village girl like me. Because of my capacity to read at lightning speed, the Reverend sisters noticed me and started nurturing my creative and leadership potentials. As a form 2 student, I underwent a mental test. The Reverend sisters challenged the form five students that I could do better than them in dictation. They took the bait and one midmorning, this was me, a form2 student sitting in class amongst big form five students with Reverend Sister Rosemary dictating to us. To this day, I do not know if it was by design or by coincidence but the

Visionary Woman

text she had chosen was from a book I had read in the library. It was set in a European countryside with words like "hedgehog," "spruce," "poplar," "birch," "wolf," "bison," and "trotting horses" baffling the form 5 students. After we were done writing, we all exchanged our scripts to carry out the corrections. I made zero mistakes. The form five students passed my script from hand to hand and gazed at it in disbelief. That huge dose of self-confidence must have made me grow two inches taller right there in front of those form 5 students.

FIRST LEADERSHIP EXAMINATIONS

When I got to form 3, my classmate came to me with a dilemma. Her father had asked her to study physics because he wanted her to go to medical school. At that time in St Bede's, the academic time table was gender sensitive. When it was time for the boys to study physics, the girls would be in the domestic science lab where they studied how to cook and bake. The girls were being prepared to be educated housewives while the boys would be the engineers and doctors to marry those educated girls. For an African girl, baking scones, cakes, shepherd's pie and all those European dishes was a novelty and we were quite happy to cook, taste those dishes, and accept the verdict of the Reverend authorities for the girls not to bother with physics. I reluctantly told my friend to stop her weeping because I was going to accompany her to study physics. I say "reluctantly" because thinking of all the European dishes I was going to miss made it a difficult choice for a 13-year-old. The first and second term results in physics were a disaster for my friend and I, but during the third term we started understanding abstract notions like the law of gravity, joules, amperes, and all the jargon that the boys used to brag about.

In form 4, my biggest leadership trial was offered to me by Reverend Father Van Bleisen who was our principal; he made me the only senior prefect (SP) for the school. Before then, there had always been a boy and girl as SPs for the school. Boys made up about three quarters of the school population. The boys felt slighted and they immediately started hatching plans to carry out a strike action. When the student body heard about it, there was tension in the air and everyone was eagerly waiting to see how the Reverend gentlemen and I would handle it. We all knew that a strike action could turn ugly. To this day, I cannot understand where the wisdom I used came from. Surely from God. I told the Reverend Father not to punish or expel the leaders of the strike action but to give me a week with them. He reluctantly agreed. I started with some "high level" talks involving only the leaders of the strike action. I remembered how my parents used to get me to do chores that were difficult just by using words that uplifted me. I told them that I needed them to help me keep order in the school and that they were way more important than me. The title of "SP" was just an empty title that would be more ridiculous if they did not help me to do the work. After three days of "intensive talks," they all agreed that gunning for the post of a boy SP was no big deal. A girl SP who was ready to let them work was cool. I went back to the principal to announce that he did not have to worry about anything. From then on, there was peace in school. I let the boy and girl prefects do their thing and I would come out once a month in the general assembly to lay out lines of conduct for the student body in "perfectly prepared addresses." I say "perfectly prepared addresses" because addressing the student body was something that my 15-year-old brain took seriously so I could move them into the right choices. Some 40 years later, students would meet me and quote from my addresses. This delegation of duties gave me time to indulge in my best pastime; reading novels and writing essays. My essays were so unique that the Reverend fathers would have me read them out so they could record on a tape recorder and send them back home to Holland. They knew that people in Holland would not believe that an African child could write such essays. With this effective leadership, I had time to study. I had A and B grades in all my papers at the GCE Ordinary Level. Up till then, almost all SPs had done poorly at the final examinations because they would spend most of their time trying to keep order in school. The boys in my class could not handle it when I had an A grade in physics, but by then we were already moving on to high school. My time in St Bede's College was the best time of my life. I was learning so many things at a really fast pace and those lessons have stayed with me till today.

BECOMING DOCTOR FON ELIZABETH

Growing up in the sixties, education for girls became the "in" thing. We girls were taught that if we went to school, got the right certificates, landed good jobs with good salaries, and got hooked to working husbands, our places in paradise were assured. Being a doctor in the seventies was a big deal. I got hooked up with a petroleum engineer and our honeymoon lasted less than a year. I woke up to reality and it was not a pleasant reality at all.

No one had taught us relationship-building skills while we were studying academic subjects. No one had taught my husband how to relate to this new African girl who is a professional, articulate, wage-earning career girl, nor me how to relate to an African boy. We held on to what our parents had taught us as we were growing up which was basically not to show your earnings to your spouse. If the marriage goes sour, no big deal. Fall back on your career and earnings.

My marriage had its share of challenges. I miscarried twice and for eight years we were unable to conceive. In Africa, where many believe having children is the only reason why people should stay in marriage, most of my days were unhappy, especially the days around my period. I remember going to work, locking myself in the toilet to cry for a few minutes before washing my face to come out to start consultations. I thank God for my friend and colleague Dr Nguimatsia Madeleine, who stood by me during those trying times with tons of empathy. Without that shoulder to cry on, I wonder where I would be today.

Working with male colleagues was something that boys and girls were not taught in school. The working landscape in Cameroon was changing rapidly. Girls were entering the workforce at a fast pace. Some of them had to supervise teams of male and female colleagues. The boys brought their traditional and cultural/religious beliefs to the workplace. No one had taught boys how to relate to a female boss and no one had taught a female boss how to relate to a male colleague. As the first female head of the Bonassama District hospital theater, I had to go through many of these funny scenarios. I would examine a lady in labour and diagnose a caesarean section. The husband would be told to come to my office so I could explain to him why I was deciding on a caesarean section for his wife. Many times, the husbands would come in and see me alone sitting behind my table and they would be like, "I have been sent here to see the doctor who is going to operate on my wife. Where is 'HE?' " and I say "HE" in quotes and in capital letters because I could just feel in the tone of their voices that they would not believe me if I said I was the doctor. I could feel a husband's brain grinding into gear as he would be asking himself if he could entrust the life of his wife into the hands of a "little girl." In his mind I was just a girl and girls were not supposed to operate on patients.

As the first female to be appointed as the District Medical Officer (DMO), supervising the activities of over three hundred doctors, nurses and support staff, it was not always easy to work with my male colleagues. I had to cross the high sea three times with my male colleagues to control epidemics in the Cap Cameroon islands. Not being a swimmer, and with the rough seas, I had to master my fear and still appear to be in control in front of my male colleagues whom I suspect were secretly praying that I should "lose" it. Thank God those days are gone and men are beginning to accept changes in the gender landscape in the workplace.

Dr Sylvia Forchap-Likambi et al

SEEDS OF THE TESHO (Team Spirit Holistic) CONCEPT ARE SOWN

In all of this toxic brew at home and at work, a new word that was unheard of in the sixties reared up its ugly head and that word became a member of every household and every work place. You guessed right, STRESS became our daily reality at home and at work.

As a medical doctor who was undergoing stress and trying to find refuge at work, I realized that my work/life balance was askew. I could not get help from my colleagues because they too were grappling with the same challenges. I could not ask my husband to go with me to see a psychiatrist because asking an African man to go with his wife to see a psychiatrist meant I saw him as a "mad" man. In our environment, a psychiatrist was and probably is still seen by many as the "mad" people's doctor. In any case, as a medical doctor, I knew that my psychiatrist colleagues had their hands full with more serious cases (3 psychiatrists for a population of two million inhabitants in the town of Douala in the year 2000). I calculated that work/life balance challenges for a medical colleague like me was not on the top of the list of their priorities.

Then, I was appointed the Regional Coordinator of the 35 centers in the Littoral where HIV/TB patients receive healthcare from some 200 doctors, nurses and support staff. The cure rate for TB in 2006 when I was appointed was a dismal 60% (40% of the patients were either lost to follow up or they were dead). I started by asking the patients why they were not coming to the centers to collect their free drugs and many felt that the healthcare providers were stigmatizing and discriminating against them. HIV/TB are two highly stigmatizing diseases in our context. The findings revealed that the greatest need of these patients besides drugs was to be UNDERSTOOD, LISTENED TO and VALUED. That was when the TESHO (Team Spirit Holistic) Program was born to create healthy relationships in a holistic way: Healthy relationships between healthcare providers and the patients, healthy relationships in the healthcare team, healthy relationships from home. We saw the need to conceive and to build the following modules amongst others:

- Non-Violent Communication (NVC) at home and at work.
- Role of team members at home and at work.
- Stages of development of children and effective parenting skills in our environment.
- Team spirit in financial management.
- Holistic Customer Care at work and at home/Expression of gratitude in relationships.
- Challenges to HIV prevention linked to couple sexuality.
- Study of the four main personality types and how to minimize the weaknesses of each personality type for team building at home and at work.
- Leadership and empathy in health personnel.

With the implementation of these TESHO skills, the TB cure rate hit the WHO target of 85% in 2015 in the Littoral Region.

SPREAD OF TESHO

By word of mouth, many groups of persons, companies, churches and families started asking for the TESHO conferences. They wanted a book that could be read in/out of Cameroon and that was how our first book titled "A Great Husband for a Great Wife" was published in 2014. A second book titled "Reconcile? No Way!" is about to be released.

There was also a need for a center where people could unburden themselves to a listening ear in order to get simple easy-to-apply life skills for their relationship challenges. The TESHO Center was created in 20016 to teach those context-appropriate relationship skills that are sorely needed in our context to mitigate the effects of stress in relationships.

Unhealthy relationships have a high spill-over effect into the health, overall wellbeing, and job performance of individuals. It is a surprise to many parents to realize in a TESHO workshop that children are little adults who secrete adrenaline when they see their parents going through storms in their marriages. Adrenaline secretion affects children the same way it affects adults; sleeplessness, palpitations, loss of appetite, drop in school performance and stress-related illnesses. Most of these children carry the scars into their future relationships. It is about time we start learning how to build healthy communities from healthy relationships. It all starts from home. It is linked to the power in a name.

Let me share part of our family journey with you. My husband and I considered our babies' names carefully before naming them because we knew that we would use those names to spur them to achieve all they would want to achieve in this life all by themselves. It is for that reason that we named our first daughter after my husband's mother and our twin boys were named Love and Hope Fon Thaddeus after their dad. They are all following in the footsteps of their dad. Love is the SP and student elder while Hope is the education prefect of their school. They both passed 11 papers at the GCE Ordinary Level all in A and B grades. We could afford to buy them toys when they were little but we refrained from doing so. Instead, we encouraged them and they proudly built their own toys. Not offering children toys came from our upbringing. That is the power in a name transmitted from generation to generation

We do not have to be rich to name a child and bring him up right. A child holds the future of our planet in that tiny body. God gives us the wisdom to bring them up right.

Dr Fon Fonong Elizabeth

TESHO CEO

Chapter Four

THE ART OF RESILIENCE

By Angela Preston

'How do you cope when faced with such loss?'

I asked my mum this question when I was sixteen, and she had just lost her youngest brother at the age of thirty-five. Loss and grief had played a huge part in my childhood; my mum was one of eight children, and by the time I reached sixteen, five of those siblings would have passed away, the youngest thirty-two and the oldest thirty-nine. By the time I got to the age of nineteen, my mum had lost the last of her brothers, leaving only herself and my aunty Mary left to wonder why and how they could have faced such heartache.

My mum's words on answering that question are the words I use when faced with any adversity or challenges I encounter throughout my life. "Ange, we don't have a choice. No matter how difficult life gets, we have to dust ourselves down and keep going." So often, I have had to hold onto those words in order to put one foot in front of the other.

Looking back on when my mum uttered those words, I know she was finding it hard to dust herself off once again after losing not only the baby of her family, but her friend who so often called to check up on her when he was out working in his taxi. He had been there to make her laugh, and here she was trying to convince me we have to be strong whatever we may be faced with, but the pain in her eyes told me otherwise. She also knew she had to keep going because of her own family.

Life can be unfair for some and incredible for others, and understanding from a young age about loss and how to deal with it has given me an inner strength that I am my mum's daughter and in tough times I go back to that sixteen-year-old and repeat those words to myself.

The first time I really had to dust myself down was after the loss of my mum when I was just thirty-five. Although I shared in my mum's pain along with my five sisters when we lost aunties and uncles, I didn't know the true pain until she left this world. Trying to find understanding in her loss was one of the most difficult experiences of my entire life. How had she come to terms with so much loss, when I couldn't even get out of bed? Those words she had uttered to me as a sixteen-year-old were nowhere to be found; I would lay there trying to form those words in my mind, praying for her to utter the words, "Hello, my Angie Pangie," (her nickname for me). The touch of her hand and the voice that made everything okay - they were all gone, and I didn't know if I would ever dust myself down again.

Visionary Woman

After six weeks of crying myself to sleep, of my children suffering and my husband not knowing how he could help me, a light came on when my friend Sandra appeared at my bedroom door to tell me to pull myself together. It was as though she came in the form of my mum when she said, "Would your mum have done this to you? Would she lock herself away in her bedroom and forget her duty as a mum?" That was the first time I really knew the true meaning of dusting yourself down and getting on with it. Her role as a parent came before everything else, so being there for my children - no matter how much pain I felt - was my job as a mum to my sons. I had to show them how they too must always dust themselves down, just as my own mum had taught me all those years before. That was what was really important.

I promised myself that day that everything I did from then on would be in my mum's memory, for the impact she had had on my life. I forever give thanks for the lady who brought me into this world, for all that she was, and all that she taught me. No matter how difficult her life was, she was never without a smile; the joy in her face when she was around her girls is a vision I still carry in my heart to this day and instead of the pain I felt for so long after her death, it is now replaced with gratitude and a profound appreciation that God blessed me with a role model whose teachings I would use for the rest of my life.

There will be many challenges and obstacles we face throughout our lives; you would have to be very lucky or live on an island alone if you were to get out of this world without facing some form of adversity but how do we get back up after falling? Dusting myself down has become part of my make-up. When we are born, we are not born to love or to hate, nor are we born with wisdom or the answers to dealing with life, but we are born with genes and lessons that are passed down from our parents, and being able to adapt and accept change - no matter how difficult - is something we can learn from past experiences we have faced. It could be the loss of a loved one as I had witnessed with my mum, the loss of a job, or the loss of a relationship; no matter what way we look at it, it is change and how we respond to that change which will define if we live another day or we give up and accept our fate.

The 10th of May 2014 is etched in my memory forever. That was the day I decided to take back control and make a decision that I didn't know if I'd live to regret but was a decision that had to be made. I was sitting on the end of my bed looking into the mirror and didn't recognise the person looking back at me. They say our eyes are the window to our souls, and my soul that day was dead, and it was the last two years and the events that had happened in that time that had caused such pain. I was very blessed to have been born with the same personality as my mum, forever smiling and laughing and looking for joy in everything, but in that moment, I couldn't find any joy in life, nor could I smile or laugh.

The job I had worked so hard for was slowly being taken away from me and all because of the actions of one person. As someone who left school with very few qualifications, I had been working for the same organisation for nearly twenty years and felt very grateful to be doing a job I loved with the bonus of a salary that gave myself and my family a life I could only have dreamt of as a child. I had worked

Visionary Woman

my way up the ranks from self-employed agent to area manager and my role included going into different locations to up-skill staff and achieve objectives, but I was left with no choice but to walk away from that role, and all because one man wanted more than I was willing to give.

In 2012 I was on a training course when I was informed this man was about to become our new divisional manager. He was a very charismatic man, and I was told by a colleague that everyone loved him and he always got what he wanted. I remember thinking, 'Oh really, I wonder what hold he has on others to be so conceited or was that just talk to make us all sit up and take him seriously?' Well, it wouldn't be long before I found out when he decided to pay me a visit in Blackburn to tell me he had heard all about the hard work I had done as a leader and the results we were getting as a team and how he could help me progress. Looking back, I thought, 'Maybe he is what people were saying about him and he is a genuine compassionate leader,' after chatting about family and things we enjoy, including the love of a society he was part of which my mother-in-law was also involved in, albeit in different parts of the UK. I thought at that time that he was actually a really nice guy who maybe I had misunderstood, a thought that I would live to regret only two years later.

The company not only paid us well for the hard work, but they also rewarded us with fantastic gifts for achieving objectives such as nights away, and not long after he had resumed the role of divisional manager the division had a night away planned in Birmingham. However, you had to achieve results in order to gain a place. For this particular one I had not met the criteria, but he insisted that I accompany them on the night. Not thinking anything of it at the time, off I went along with one of my development managers to enjoy a night at the Theatre, a meal and a few drinks, and that was to be the beginning of the end when I refused a night cap back at the hotel.

For the next two years this man made my life hell; he called me derogatory words in front of others, put me down, insisted I sing happy birthday to one of the senior managers in a Marilyn Munroe tone in a room filled with both men and women, and finally he decided he was going to move his office into my location, after putting me through a disciplinary that would not have stood up in a company with integrity, an audit that he had arranged within a day. It was the worry of him moving into my location that sent fear right through my body, the words I had heard two years before - 'he gets what he wants' - was all I could think about, and the only thing left for me to do was walk away from the only life I knew.

I didn't know whether I would lose my house because of the loss of income, or my mind, but I was not losing my dignity nor was I going to be a plaything for someone who thought he could treat women with such little regard that all they were was commodities to him.

As I sat on the bed and looked into that mirror, it was my mum's voice that I heard loud and clear: "Ange we don't have a choice, no matter how difficult life gets, we have to dust ourselves down and keep going," and that is what I would do after leaving a job I had skipped into and felt so grateful to be doing for all those years.

It was either give in or walk away and the latter was the only thing I could do; it wasn't just my mum's words but showing my children that when something no longer serves you, it is time to walk away, no matter how difficult the decision is.

For six weeks after going off sick, just as before when losing my mum, I took to my bed and didn't know where my life would go, but in my heart, I always knew I had made the right decision. As difficult as it was, the determination to prove to this company I wouldn't take it lying down was all that went through my mind. After giving in my notice in May and deciding I wanted to become a motivational speaker, my husband printed off all the literature on how to accomplish it. I did not want anyone else to go through what I had been through and wanted to ensure anyone I met who was faced with adversity or obstacles, they would have the tools to overcome them, but I wasn't really sure where to start. I even toyed with the idea of training to be a human rights lawyer but felt too old. Here I was at forty-six and terrified about having to change my whole life due to one self-obsessed individual.

But now I was in bed and the idea of being a motivational speaker was the last thing on my mind; my only thought at that time was ending my life. I felt like a failure. I was lost and I was angry that I had been put in a position that meant I had no income, and not really sure if I would ever be capable of earning one again. It was a holiday to Egypt that my husband had booked which brought me to my senses and the fight back first started. When he said, "Why don't you write a book?" The idea was laughable - who would want to read my book? I was a kid from a council estate in Liverpool with no great story to share (or so I thought). It's funny how things come back to you when you most need it. When I was a little girl, my sister always called me Hans Christian Anderson because I always had a story to tell and now I was thinking, could I write a book? So there and then I started writing my first book, 'Opening Doors', a story that was first written as my thoughts and as a tool to help me deal with the events of the past two years. Never in my wildest dreams did I expect to support thousands and help them realise the true art of resilience and how to find it in the most difficult of times.

Only on returning from holiday and reading the literature on how to become a motivational speaker did I realise that to stand out from the crowd, writing a book and sharing my knowledge as well as my experiences was what I needed to do in order to achieve my end goal. Research started with Google and following the instructions of a man with a name similar to my mum's is what would lead me onto the path of becoming a published author: Joseph Campbell, a writer and philosopher, whose teachings I would use as a sign from my mum that her words of dusting myself down were right there in front of me. She was christened Josephine Campbell and the message on the computer screen was enough for me to realise I was meant to be where I was and sharing my message was all I could think about.

Knowing why you want to achieve a goal is the key to never letting obstacles or curveballs get in your way, and going back to that little girl, watching my mum as she continued to put one foot in front of the other each time she lost a sibling, would be the foundation on which I would move forward. When faced with a challenge, we must find the courage and the inner strength to overcome it, and that comes from learning, growing, and observing how others do it before us. Our purpose here is to learn to teach others how they too can use past experiences as a stepping stone to help them become the person they were born to be, and that includes all the difficult times too.

Failure and fear had turned into hope and determination to use my experiences to help me in my quest to become the motivational speaker I had so wanted after watching an incredible man, who had been hired by the company a couple of years earlier to inspire us all to look at new ways to develop. He spoke about magic dust - that magic dust is self-belief, and we all have it within us – and again, relating it to my mum, it was all I needed to hear. All these signs were aligning themselves with where I was meant to be, and this is the thing about the significance of change. If we are able to flip it over and see the positive in it, we are able to identify the meaning within that change in order to benefit ourselves so as to make new choices, ones that will also impact others through the decisions we make.

After deciding I would actually publish the book, I gave myself one year to achieve that; my point of not just laying down and taking it would be profound in the action I took. If we use bad times as a way to look to the future, the chances of failing will be minimal, and at that time, that is what I did to ensure the book was published within the timeframe. I still look back at this time and feel my mum and dad were pushing me forward and urging me on when the days became tough. I'm not saying it's easy - it is actually the hardest thing to do when you get back up after falling - but once you have fallen so far down, there is only ever one way to go and that is back to the top. Revenge was never what I ever wanted as I am also a forgiving person, but I did feel a sense of power that would give me the courage to keep striving and wanting more.

The realization that things I thought impossible before were now possible gave me the belief that dreams do come true if you know what your purpose is. Had I not gone through that dreadful experience I would not be living a purposeful life, one that not only feeds my soul but also one that gives courage to others to realise their own potential. From this one experience I have used the teachings from my mum to overcome a challenge that I thought had broken me and used it to spur me on to live life on my terms; and we all have it within us to do the same.

After achieving my goal of publishing 'Open Doors', the interest was so big that it made it all the way to America and standing in Times Square in September 2016 signing books and being interviewed in Guggenheim Productions really was what dreams are made of. Just two years after being on the floor after a breakdown, here I was surrounded by Americans who couldn't wait to read my story - a story that I thought wasn't interesting, yet these people had queued to buy my book and chat with me about the content within this book. I had to pinch myself so many times to check whether I was dreaming and kept looking at my husband to see the joy in his eyes that his wife had fought hard to overcome yet another challenge, all whilst awaiting the publication of my second book, 'The Keys To Success In Business', a book based on the characters of a leader, the character we all possess within. Before leading anyone, we first must lead ourselves and this book was written to support others in the belief that they too are leaders, and that nothing is out of reach when we work hard and believe in our own abilities.

My biggest battles and the most difficult times as well as my greatest pleasures will always be those of a mum, and it is in this role that I miss the wise words of my mum who taught me not only how to carry myself as a woman, but the most important job of all: that of a mum. When I brought my eldest son into the world, it was his appearance that gave me that need to build a life where opportunities were open to him but being the mum my own had been was what was most important to me. As a parent to three sons, life was never going to be easy, but I had the knowledge, the armor, and the wisdom to start me off and it was up to me to remember those teachings and use that wisdom to pave the way for my own children to grow and develop as they forged their own way in this world.

Each of my sons have their own personality just as I and my sisters have, but all of them were always very loving children who never finished a conversation without us telling each other how much we are all loved. We created a loving home with an open approach where discussions about our days would be heard every day at the dinner table, and Friday was always film night where we gathered around the TV for family time, myself and my husband on one settee and my three sons on the other. I so often look back at these times and wish they could have been frozen in time so I could have protected my youngest from the horrors that awaited him. Setting my son's up in a home where they felt loved and secure in the knowledge that they could be anything was all that I ever wanted, and both myself and Barry worked tirelessly to ensure this happened.

As the years went on my sons' personalities were formed, and their ambitions of what they wanted from life would show themselves in all their glory. Christopher always said he would be a millionaire by the time he was 35, and he wanted his first car to be a Mazda; he wasn't sure what he wanted to do, but money somehow became his motivation. Leighton was a very sensitive child and from five his dream to be a police officer was all he ever thought of; when he played the game of cops and robbers with his brothers and cousin Kieran, he was always the police officer. Then there was Joseph, who loved hearing the stories of both his grandads who had been in the Kings Regiment together and his dream was to follow in their footsteps. After leaving school, all my sons went off to work in America in summer camps; I ensured they had the chances I didn't. As a family with six girls, my mum and dad didn't have the money to give us such opportunities, but I ensured my children got to realise the world was accessible and they didn't need to settle for anything.

After returning from California at nineteen, Christopher decided to move to London to give himself the opportunities that weren't available in Liverpool; he has worked hard to achieve his goals and is now a top businessman in quantitative finance and risk management, living the dream he set as a child with a beautiful wife Gemma and the blessing of a wonderful son Maxwell. Christopher's strength of mind and determination to realise his dream had been there from a child, and seeing him happy meant I knew our job as parents was done. Witnessing how they are both creating a strong family foundation for my grandson to grow brings the biggest joy to my heart.

Visionary Woman

Leighton went off to university to study law and education to help him in his quest to become a police officer; in between this, just as Christopher had before him, he went off to America, choosing New York to work at a camp. Every summer from the age of eighteen to twenty-four this little quiet, sensitive boy went backwards and forwards to build the character that would see him living his dream of becoming a police officer, today he is one of the youngest in service to make sergeant, with his sights set on one day becoming a gold commander; I know that dream will happen due to his ambition to serve others.

Joseph, whose intelligence was off the scale, left school with nineteen GCSEs and a Business Diploma; the opportunities that awaited him could not be measured, but his dream of joining the army was all he ever spoke about. Every conversation we had about the army, I felt my heart fall further, and I prayed he'd change his mind; the thought of him going off to fight in a war sent fear right through my body. I had grown up watching the troubles in Northern Ireland and British Soldiers being killed was all I worried about for my own son, but today when I think back, I often wonder if Joseph's dream had come true would his life have been different. He had fought for his life from the minute he was conceived; he was a twin and we lost one before the birth of Joseph, so his fighting spirit was there from day one.

At sixteen Joseph's dream was shattered when he was refused access to the army due to eczema; the relief I felt was not felt by Joseph as he was devastated that his dream had not come true. Looking back, I was selfish to wish for this because this was the catalyst for Joseph's downfall, and his mental health took a downward spiral. He saw his brothers living their dream lives and working towards their end goals and in his eyes he had disappeared in the blink of an eye. By the time he was eighteen, he decided to follow in the footsteps of his big brothers, and off he went to New York to work in a camp. I had seen a glimpse of the old Joseph and hoped this would be a turning point, but as a mum I couldn't help but worry about him; I knew he wasn't made of the same stuff as Christopher and Leighton - he was more fragile and waving him off my heart once again felt heavy. I wished the days away for him to return home.

On his return, he seemed to have newfound hope but, as before he went away, it didn't last long, and his problems would present themselves so many times. As the years have gone on my worry for Joseph and being able to tap into that resilient mindset my beautiful mum taught me thirty-eight years ago is something I sometimes find very difficult to do, but no matter how many times Joseph falls I will forever be there to pick him up until he's ready to lift himself up, just as I will for all three of my sons if they need me. So many times, I have gone to bed praying for another day for Joseph and woke up praying. My prayers have been answered and God has spared him. I have to keep the hope in my heart that one day he will recover from his illness of addiction and mental illness.

My work that I believe I was led to is working with those in recovery from addiction and is what keeps me going. I know in my heart the day will come when Joseph is working alongside me to offer support to those who, like him, have lost their way in life and need that helping hand to find their way back.

It is my biggest pain that keeps me going and if I can give anyone reading this any advice on how to find and understand the art of resilience: think of your worst pain - what lessons can you learn from it? How can you benefit from it, but more importantly how will you act on it so others can benefit from it? Also, rewrite your story; never leave the pen in someone else's hand, take back control, and learn from the lessons you are being shown. I feel grateful for all the challenges I have faced as they have given me the strength and the courage to keep fighting and being present for all of my children and those who need support to live the life they were born for.

My life's work now includes four published books, my fifth nearing publication, a play titled "A Time To Leave" which was staged in 2018, a Ted-X talk on resilience, and studying Politics and Creative Writing in Liverpool Hope University in order to continue serving. As well as my work in recovery I also run programs in schools to divert children away from criminality and build the necessary tools to lead positive, productive lives and all of this came because my need to keep rising after falling is greater than the need to stay down and my mum's words are always at the forefront of my mind.

"Never let anyone tell you it can't be done, show them it can" - Unknown

By Angela Preston - Author of Opening Doors

Chapter Five

DIAMOND SHARPENS DIAMOND

By Neva Brooks

At the beginning of the global Covid-19 pandemic, at the time of uncertainty and unrest across the world, I had the audacity to step out on faith and birth a vision God planted inside me. I'd ascribed to the words in Habakkuk 2:2 to "write the vision and make it plain" several years prior to the pandemic. Only God knew that this vision would come forth during the pandemic. I remember vividly asking God, "Father, is it time? Is it now?" He held my hand and gently told me "Yes, it's time to push." It was like being in the birthing room, the labour room, when delivering new life. The name *Diamonds Sharpen Diamonds* was solidified. I was at a gas station one afternoon and he spoke to me so profoundly, I opened my phone and recorded all the thoughts and words he gave me. Even now when I listen to the replay, it gives me chills.

Diamonds are one of the hardest natural surfaces known to man. Natural surface. This means it is the way God made it, the way he planned it. Another natural surface which has stood the test of time is iron. It occurs naturally by itself and in part with other minerals. It is thought to be the core of the earth! Diamonds and Iron share in common, the strength and natural components of what God intended them to be. Because of this, I understand why my vision was set in diamonds and centred on Proverbs 27:17 NLT; "As iron sharpens iron, so one person sharpens another." I believed God led me to this particular verse and chapter to understand the importance of women coming together to uphold, uplift, support and collaborate with each other. Not compete with one another but to collaborate. In doing this, we will naturally sharpen each other. As a young lady, the word I heard from the women's circle in my church was "edify." The word *edify* basically means to uplift, build, enlighten, and improve. As I began to share my vision and how God was unfolding the details, a mentor challenged me. She encouraged me to be certain my declaration of diamonds sharpening diamonds was the empirical truth. Not needing confirmation of what God said about Proverb 27:17, I set out to prove that diamonds do in fact, sharpen diamonds. I went to my local jeweler. She is part of a family I have known for years and has assisted me in repairing and designing custom pieces. I simply asked her if diamonds sharpen diamonds. Her first word was "absolutely!"

Over the next hour or so, she spoke of my vision as if she was on a conference call with me and God! From that vision, the writing of the vision on the paper, the pouring of the nataph God gave me at the gas station, she affirmed so much to me. Toward the end of our conversation, she asked to be excused for a minute. I sat waiting for her to come back and reflecting on some of the things she said when I made mental notes of specific gems she dropped. She returned and told me to hold out my hand. This woman placed a single, loose, $15,000 diamond in the centre of my palm and asked, "Can you feel that?" My mentor had no idea sending me on the quest to prove a point would change my life.

Over the course of this concourse, I will share with you how being a visionary woman of God has changed my life and the lives of others.

Diamonds Sharpen Diamonds™ is designed for women. This is a space we hold for our sisterhood to share and receive. The mission statement for Diamonds Sharpen Diamonds™ is: "Uplifting, Honouring, and Supporting each other through LOVE, LISTENING, RESPECT and CONFIDENTIALITY." Currently, the platform is virtual and will soon include in-person conferences and workshops. We have sponsored live Zoom workshops, podcasts, and private sessions at the "polishing table," which I will tell you more about later. This vision for uplifting and supporting women has reached 25 of the states and territories in the United States and also spread to Australia, Jamaica, Africa, Europe, China, Japan, and Canada. I must say I had no idea when God said to push at the beginning of a pandemic, it would open the door to national, international and global connections resulting in a sisterhood and bond between Diamonds all over the world. Every day I am grateful I didn't abort the vision, I listened to the voice of God for the right nurturing of the vision, I honour my heavenly father and want to publicly say, he gets the glory!

From the vision, seeds have grown. While most of the interactions with Diamonds sharpening other Diamonds happened in group settings in public and private settings, there grew a need to have other means of touching and supporting. Women began to form partnerships and collaborate on initiatives to reach other women. This was oftentimes taking a concept from Diamond sessions or workshops and duplicating them in their social groups, families, and churches. More and more women asked for a private one-on-one session with me. In these times together, we sharpened each other to become better and stronger individuals. Self-care, forgiving ourselves and others, releasing the old not-so-good habits, and declaring new ways to effectively move forward became encouraging and empowering conversations.

I began to read powerful books and spend time with mentors who poured into my life and encouraged me, as I encouraged others.

In her book *What I Meant to Say* Dr. Cindy Bailey writes:

> "Someone will always be prettier. They will be smarter. Their house will be larger. They will drive a better car. Their children will do better in school. Their husband will fix more things around the house. So, let it go and love you and your circumstances. Think about it, the prettiest woman in the world can have hell in her heart. The most highly favored woman on your job may be unable to have children. And the richest woman you know…she's got the house, the car and the clothes, and just might be lonely."

Visionary Woman

Sometimes you have to encourage and motivate yourself! I want you to reflect on your position in life right now. This is an introspective view of you! Some "she" is always going to *appear* to be, have, and do more, much like Dr. Cindy said. But what about you?

Take a few minutes to reflect and write three ways you can encourage yourself:

_____

_____

_____

As a woman, a visionary who is able to see beyond your physical sight, are you encouraging and being encouraged? Are you open to positive, constructive feedback or are you uncomfortable in a place of stagnant complacency?

Diamond Sharp Coaching, LLC

From these types of conversations, I felt the need to push, again. God was increasing my ability to see on a larger scale. He showed me that my vision was nearsighted and in order to serve the women he assigned to me, I must envision a greater scope. The vision to walk with women from a point of being stuck to moving to a better place. In other words, the ability to see what is happening up close as well as envision what can be in the distance! At this time, I had been a Licensed Registered Nurse for more than 30 years. In the field of nursing, I found my love and expertise in Psychiatry, Behavioural Health, Mental Wellness. During this time I served in capacities from the bedside to the boardroom. All along the way, I knew there was more for me to do. I could sense the unfinished work in me.

Outside of the biblical reference in Habakkuk 2:2 to "write the vision," the hospital was the first time I was challenged to actually take pen to paper to write down my vision. The hospitals had vision and mission statements and encouraged us to develop our individual statements relative to theirs. This is an exercise where we may all take part! Writing your vision as it relates to your passion, your inspirations and your dreams can be a game changer in activating your vision.

Back during the pandemic, a colleague extended a partnership proposal, and I joined the concept of offering multiple mental wellness services under one roof. Think about the big box stores where you can do one-stop shopping. I apologize if that triggered some Black Friday nightmares! Full disclosure, I'm aware that not everyone enjoys box-store shopping. However, this coaching thing came up again and I had the opportunity to coach in an environment conducive to uplifting, honouring, and supporting clientele through listening, respect, and confidentiality. Does that sound familiar? It is the unfolding of the vision to serve!

I became a Certified Life Coach and founded Diamond Sharp Coaching, LLC. God gave me a vision for the coaching business and settled this scripture in my heart:

"For we walk by faith, not by sight." 2 Corinthians 5:7

"Ladies, How Are You Walkin'?"

We walk by faith and not by sight

Visionary Woman

Are you walking by faith with your shoes too tight?

You know you need a 9 but you are squeezing that 8…

You best get the right size before it's everlasting too late!

Sis, you know that shoe really ain't your size

So stop right now, quit telling yourself those lies!

God didn't give you that assignment you chose if for yourself

You said he gave it to you 'cause it look good on someone else

Walk on by faith my sister, you are who HE designed

Go ahead woman of God, Be comfortable in your size 9!

I wrote this poem, and it has become a favourite among the Diamonds I serve. I walk with creative, professional, women from points of conflict in their lives to places of clarity and freedom. My coaching niche is nurses. This fits well with my experience and the reliability is conducive to individual and group coaching. I am a nurse, and I get it. Every single woman I've worked with is creative. I'm serious about that! I don't recall a time I went beyond the second meeting with a woman without her discovering some level of creativity. It is in us, it is purpose, it is God given, it IS VISION! It is you!

The Oxford Languages Dictionary describes vision in part as: "the ability to think about or plan the future with imagination or wisdom." Sis, that is YOU! How many times a day do you do this? Planning for tomorrow's dinner takes vision. The ability to remain in a healthy, fulfilling relationship, be it marriage or partnership, requires

Dr Sylvia Forchap-Likambi et al

vision. Charting the path for your children's education and growth is led by creativity and vision for certain.

Envisioning the 4 Cs

One of the brightest facets in the vision God gave me for Diamond Sharp coaching has been the 4 Cs. They are in alignment with the process of becoming a Diamond: Conflict, Cut, Carat and Clarity. Walk with me as we compare and contrast the model with the life of a diamond and the visionary life of a "Diamond Sister."

Conflict

The Diamond starts as a piece of carbon and goes through an enormous amount of time, heat and pressure. According to the British Jeweller's Association, natural diamonds are more than 900 million years old. The oldest known diamond is 3 billion years old. It is believed the right conditions for diamonds to be created are at temperatures of 1,600 to 2,300 degrees Fahrenheit and 650,000 and 850,000 psi. To put this in perspective, the average human body core temperature is about 98.6 degrees Fahrenheit. PSI is an abbreviation for pounds per square inch. In my SUV, the recommended psi for my tires is 33psi. Ponder that. 1,600 degrees vs 98.6 degrees. The next time you go for a drive, check the inside door panel to find your recommended psi.

Women also undergo the time, heat and pressures of life. Time is a commodity we can never claim again! "You must effectively utilize the time you have been blessed with while here on Earth… for every second gone, we will never be able to get it back, so too are the amazing opportunities gone with it! Arise and take action while you still have the time to do so." This is the way Dr. Sylvia Forchap-Likambi puts it. In her book "Success Blueprint," there are valuable gems to help us identify and accomplish success in gaining clarity in life.

Yes, certainly we go through transitions which can be quite difficult and challenging. It may seem as if you will NEVER get clarity and the conflict you are in will never end. May I encourage you to view the time in your challenge the way Dr Sylvia suggests? There may be tears and pain right now, but remember joy will follow in the morning! Psalm 30:5. There can be advantages of growing and going through the heat and pressure. The diamond isn't being consumed by the heat and pressure, not at all. In fact, it is quite the contrary! The diamond is being made strong and solid. Protected by each layer of conflict, the diamond becomes more resilient and internally more beautiful! I have three tips for you Diamond. They will help strengthen you in conflict:

1. Look at the situation as a challenge instead of a threat. Make short term goals and take each day one at a time until you can handle bigger tasks. You will get stronger each day. Stay focused.

2. Visualize yourself succeeding. Remember our talk about encouraging yourself? Now is the time to make the time to

think back on previous occasions when you overcame a difficult heat and pressure.

3. Reward yourself often in ways you appreciate. This can be as small as a cup of your favourite tea, a walk around the block or treating yourself to a massage or your favourite dinner.

Years ago, I saw one of my elders boil potatoes and eggs in the same water to make potato salad. I didn't think much of it at the time. Later in life I heard someone say the water that boils potatoes to make them soft, is the same water that boils eggs and makes them hard. The heat and time in the pot may be the same; it is what's on the inside that determines the outcome! You have vision inside you. You have purpose inside you. You have greatness inside you! Whatever you do, use your time wisely when you go through heat and pressure. Time is one commodity we can't get back.

Cut

Diamonds are formed about 100 miles below the earth's core. It took the eruption of volcanoes to release a substance called magna with the diamonds embedded in it. Once the diamonds are mined, there is a cutting process to remove the outer layers of the conflict they've made it through. Skilled diamond cutters carefully remove the excess to reveal the diamond. Multi cuts or facets are made in order to allow the light from the inside to shine through.

This stage in my Diamond life caused disputes and I've experienced losses. I am grateful for Hebrews 12:1 and I'll explain. I worked to a breakthrough in life, and I truly thought people in my association would have been supportive. You know what I mean? Happy for me and ready to celebrate with me. I say my association because I realized some folk, who I thought were my friends, were not friendly. The cut…was deep. Decisions were made around me and about me of which I had no control; they hurt my feelings. I can say that today, but at the time I wore a "smiling face" mask. I wasn't okay. I didn't have it all together like I said. Even after my breakthrough, I was broken, and I lied about how I felt. The less support I received, the more I desired it. I found myself slipping back into that place of bondage.

Pastor Rosemary Jackson-Moore wrote a book titled *Taking Off the MASKS, Telling Our Story and Giving God the Glory*. She says "in the end, no matter what you call it and no matter what purpose it serves for you, a mask by any other name is still a mask." This resonates so strongly in my soul! I came out of bondage with a mask on! How dare I do that to the power of God who delivered me. Yes, I said earlier I worked my way to a breakthrough and that is true. It was work and God was merciful to deliver me.

Come here now Hebrews 12:1 "Let us strip off every weight that slows us down, especially the sin that so easily trips us up. And let us run with endurance the race God has set before us." The cutting and the stripping. The first thing to go was the mask! I got honest with myself and those around me. It cost me relationships and money. However, I gained more light with each cut! Just like the diamond, I began to let the light of Christ shine through me. I was on my way to clarity. On my way to being the rare Diamond God created me to be. On my way to gaining endurance to carry out the vision God has given me. Don't shy away from the cut. It's worth the light!

Carat

The diamond still remains one of the most beautiful stones in the world. The larger a diamond's carat weight, the more it tends to add value to the stone. Diamonds larger than a few carats are rare. Most of us will find diamonds from a quarter of a carat (0.25) to 2 carats or more. Did you know most diamonds mined today are too small or of lesser quality, and they never make it in a ring, necklace, or earrings? Smaller "chips" are sometimes used as fillers or around bigger stones. NewScientist News Magazine Issue 2765 has an article with the title *Diamond chips to make meaner, greener electronics* writes about diamond chips being used in electronics as an electrical insulator. Crushed diamonds are used for tool bits.

True confession, have you ever given back a diamond ring? What about trading it up for a bigger carat, or to get to a .50 carat?

My jeweler, who I told you about earlier, showed me a couple of videos of jewelers in India cutting and polishing beautiful diamonds. Guess what they were using…a diamond sharpening wheel. The wheel was coated and embedded with crushed diamonds! That was the proof I needed; diamonds do sharpen diamonds!

The major point here is that you are a Diamond. We are all Diamonds as I see it. Some of us are different carats, and various weights. Yet we all have value and purpose which means we are moved and motivated by vision, not by sight! You have VALUE.

V = Visionary

A = Appreciated

L = Leader

U = Unique

E = Extraordinary

I found value in this portion of *Taking off the Mask* and I hope it helps you as well. "I am going from victim to victor as God turns my messes into messages, my tears into testimonies, my trials into triumphs, and my pain into gain. I have gone from just surviving to thriving. It still amazes me how God has used my story for His glory."

Here is another example of embracing vision as opposed to being moved by what I see. Walking the journey with adult women, I realized the importance of making an impact on their daughters and other young ladies. Diamond Sharp Coaching, LLC has a 6-week offering for young ladies ages 10-15. It is the G.E.M. Girls Empowered and Motivated program. A large portion of the program addresses self-esteem and we discuss self-esteem boosters and busters each week. We establish power words at our first session and by the end of week 3, they have created positive affirmation statements based on their power words. One of their favorite activities is 'Mirror Mirror" where we talk about what and who they see in the mirror and then list ways they value and honor themselves.

Clarity = Clear Vision

Ah, the polishing table!

My jeweler always has a polishing cloth close by. Whether it's to wipe the face of a watch, a gold necklace, or a diamond, it is within reach. I asked her if there was something special about the finish on the cloth that helped to polish the jewelry. She helped me understand it is called a polishing cloth but the actual polishing of the diamond is done by the jeweler with a tool. If it isn't done carefully and correctly, the diamond could be ruined. Polish lines, nick marks, and abrasions can happen at the polishing table resulting in a lower-quality diamond. The work of coming through the conflict, having the boldness to make necessary adjustments, and finding your worth or value can be rewarding. This final step of polishing can determine the success of an individual. Early on I thought each time I was with a Diamond, we would work through each of the 4 C steps in my model. I had to repent and apologize to a few Diamonds for rushing the process and trying to determine the outcome for them before they were ready. As their coach, I was making nick marks and polishing lines in the wonderful work they'd accomplished.

Once again, I'd like to encourage you. As you sharpen and polish other Diamonds be mindful of the process of polishing. Be prayerful and careful as you serve others, always aware that one of us may plant a seed, another may water the seed, and it is God who gives the increase. Don't rush the polishing process.

Visionary Woman

This is a closing opportunity to reflect on where you are in the journey from conflict to clarity. This is your book, your time to put your thoughts and feelings to pen and paper.

The Conflict: I recognize there is a conflict that shows up in the time, heat, and pressure in my life. It may be small or great, but this is it.

1) _____
_____
_____

The Cut: These are the things I may need to eliminate from my life:

1) _____
_____
_____

These are the things I definitely need to cut to achieve clarity:

1) _____
_____
_____

The Carat: "I am" Affirmation Statements about my value:

1) _____
_____
_____

2) _____
_____
_____

3) _____
   _____
   _____

The Clarity: These goals are in line with my vision:

1) Today I will…
   _____
   _____
   _____

2) In one week I will…
   _____
   _____
   _____

3) In one month I will…
   _____
   _____
   _____

As a visionary, I pray this has helped you to see beyond your current circumstances. It doesn't really matter if things are going well, or not so well. It is imperative to acknowledge where you are now, envision where you want to be, then resolve, or cut away, barriers to manifesting the reality of your vision.

Can you see it? Can you hear it? Can you feel it? Do you smell it? Can you touch it? Ah, vision coming into focus as a reality!

Thank you for taking this walk with me from conflict to clarity. It is my prayer for you to truly walk in clarity, without hesitation and unmasked. When you find yourself in a conflict, may you always be strengthened to envision your destiny, write the vision and work your way to clarity. May you have the boldness to cut away unhealthy and unproductive things/people that diminish your value and dull your clarity.

I will close with our Diamond Affirmation. Please write it on a sticky note and put it on your mirror. Say it to yourself until you memorize and mean it. Envision yourself walking in strength, power, freedom, and clarity. Then say it with conviction to your sisters:

"You are a rare Diamond. You are precious in God's sight and my sister; I LOVE the way you shine!" Neva Brooks

Chapter Six

FINDING MYSELF

By Blanka Volna

I was naked, standing in the bathroom of our shared flat, staring at the person in the mirror. I recognised the hair, the teeth, eyes, mouth, the whole body looked somehow familiar, but that person looking back at me wasn't me anymore. All those were just bodily parts connected to the whole. I, Blanka, have dissociated from my own body because there was so much pain in my life and unexpressed grief from all the loss I have encountered in the past month. To protect myself from more pain, I have escaped from my body. You see, I was "Miss Independent," able to do everything by myself, the first-generation expat in London, living with a boyfriend, and having an OK job. I might have looked solid and robust from the outside, but inside I was crumbling and feeling abandoned, betrayed, lost, and forgotten.

There wasn't a day back then when I wouldn't think about dying and ending it all. I mean, I lost it all, one by one: I lost the man I loved so much that I moved to another country for him. I lost my job, which I was so proud of having shortly after as I was struggling to even function and serving demanding customers in a cafe became simply too much, and we had to leave the flat which I've called our home for the past one year. There was no solid ground anymore. I felt like drowning, like the biggest failure. What to do next? How to get out? What if I just end it all and stop being a burden to others? What have I done with my life? How did I even get here? As I thought these thoughts, tears streamed down my face. I was trying so hard to be everything to everyone else that I lost myself. Like Velcro, I left my dreams behind and attached myself to the person that mattered the most in my life - J. And now he was gone. And I was back to square one. Alone. I was staring in the mirror, not recognising the person looking back at me.

I was coming back to the harsh reality, realizing that focusing on what we want can be challenging, especially if you, like me, were brought up on fairy tales of submissive girls waiting for the boys to save us. That was my childhood reality, and I loved watching those stories. They were full of love and certainty, and everyone always knew what to do. Good-hearted people were always getting what they wanted, falling in love, and living happily ever after. Unfortunately, as I learned, following someone else's vision and making compromises to make the other person happy is not the key to lasting success. I lost myself by shutting down my intuition, waiting for something to happen, being passive, expecting someone or something - partner/job/parents/material things/holidays - to make me happy and fulfilled. I came to the crossroad where after a whole year of not speaking up for myself, holding onto this illusion of what I thought was love, I had to make a choice. Asking myself the most important and challenging question: What do I want?

The answers were not coming to me easily. Part of me just wanted to run and hide and get out. But where? This was all new to me, and I was still processing everything. The deadline for leaving the flat was looming above my head. Of course, there was the easy option: leave. Go back to my home country, the Czech Republic, defeated. But I'm not someone who gives up that easily. When I came to London, I had a dream bigger than myself: I wanted to build a new life for myself, to have freedom and peace. Be independent. As I was standing there, my vision started to come back to me slowly, and suddenly I knew what I had to do. You see, part of the reason for leaving the Czech Republic was because I wanted to get away from a scarcity environment. I wanted to go and see the world, be somewhere where I can provide for myself, where I don't need to ask anyone for anything, where I do not need anyone.

So, after many phone calls with my parents, sleepless nights, and mornings with tear-soaked pillows, we put together a rescue plan: my dad and sister would come to London for a visit and then help me to move back home. However, something within me was protesting against this plan. That little voice within me, which I had abandoned for a whole year, started to grow stronger. Yes, I might have come to London for love, following someone else's vision, because at only 20 years old I thought that's what you did as a good girlfriend. I mean, my mum was always the one making sacrifices in our family, and from the outside, it looked like her strategy was working. After all, my parents were still living together. So maybe if I'm a good girlfriend, move to a different country, and make my partner happy, it will work out for me too?

I'm sorry for bursting your bubble, but no. That's not how it works. If you live your life on other people's terms, making sacrifices, being the peacemaker, putting other people first with the hope that one day it will all pay off, please stop. Right now. You are hurting yourself the same as I did. And think long and hard, or even take out your journal and write down this one question: "What do I want?" Focus on you for once. Only you. At the end of the day, you are the most important person in your own life. Trust me, I know that it's easier said than done.

Such a simple question: What do I want? If you've never asked this question yourself before, or if you used to be told off by your parents for asking about what you wanted as a child, this task will be challenging. But challenging does not equal impossible; it's just a new skill that might need a bit more practice because guess what? Our mind loves what is familiar and doesn't like what is unfamiliar. Unfamiliar and new are scary. Familiar and old is safe and comfortable, and let's just stay there, please. After all, it's called the comfort zone for a reason.

Please be patient and kind to yourself, take your time, and practice asking, "What do I want?" Start with small tasks such as asking yourself, "What do I want for lunch today?" If you are always the one "having whatever the other person is having because they know better," then the next time you go to a restaurant, pick one item which you fancy from the menu. Experiment and open yourself up to making those choices, and see how different you feel. The first step to changing your life is gaining awareness and accepting the fact that you are not happy with your current situation. The next one is to stop blaming everyone and everything else and instead take full responsibility for our own lives. And start making those choices for ourselves.

Mistakes are learning opportunities, and they are part of life and the way we learn. So, when my family came for that London visit, ready to help me pack and move back home with them, I said no. I set my mind on staying, working, and studying. As much as I was scared of this new direction for my life, I was excited to follow my vision, my dreams, and my new future. I didn't know how I was going to do it, but I knew what I wanted to do. I set my mind on becoming a psychologist and started my research.

Okay, I have my vision, and it's huge and overwhelming and scary. Now what? This is what works for me: start from the end goal, backtrack, and break it down into smaller, more manageable chunks. Let me give you an example: I wanted to become an occupational psychologist, which is someone that works for companies and helps those companies improve their revenue by helping their employees and teams to work more efficiently and better overall. To do this type of job, you have to have a master's degree in Occupational Psychology. The precondition for an MSc Occupational Psychology degree is to complete a BSc Psychology course with at least a 2:1 mark, and the BSc in Psychology can be studied full-time or part-time at various universities. To study BSc Psychology in the United Kingdom as a foreign student whose first language is not English, you need to have achieved a particular overall mark in your IELTS exam. To prepare yourself for sitting the IELTS exam, you need to either attend a specific course or self-study and prepare yourself for taking the exam in 5 categories – speaking, writing, reading articles and graphs, listening, and filling in missing words. Generally speaking, the time taken to prepare each student for their IELTS exam is between 3 to 6 months.

Cool, I had my first milestone: get myself ready to sit the IELTS exam and achieve seven as the overall mark in order to be admitted to my chosen university – Birkbeck College, the University of London - for a part-time evening BSc Psychology course starting in October 2011 because in my vision, I can work and study.

And that's exactly what I did. First, I completed my IELTS with a 7.5 overall mark. Next, I wrote my letter to the university and was admitted for my four-years-long part-time BSc Psychology degree. In October 2011, while working shifts in a coffee shop to cover my bills, I started my BSc journey.

"Nothing is impossible; the word itself says I'm possible." – Audrey Hepburn

I have met many wonderful people while at Uni, made new friends, and spent countless hours, evenings, weekends, and bank holidays studying, reading articles, and writing essays and lab reports. I made so many sacrifices: my social life became non-existent, and I was spending the majority of my time between work, the gym, lecture halls, and the university library. My days usually started with getting up at 5 AM, taking a bus to work, getting the shop ready to open at 6 am for our first customers, doing my 8-hour shift, and then going home or to Uni to study. I was drinking insane amounts of coffee - the perks of working in those coffee shops - surviving on sandwiches and food which didn't get sold. I'm not going to lie, this part of my London journey was tough. When that alarm rang in the morning at 5 AM, I had to push myself out of bed, get dressed, leave the house and catch the morning bus to work. I hated my alarm clock with passion, but I didn't allow myself to slack and was diligent in my work ethic. For my studies. I had this vision, which was keeping me going, and I knew that I was getting closer, day by day, one essay at a time.

And then one day it happened: Just before lunch hour - our busiest time - I burnt out, let my emotions take over at work, caused a scene with my manager, and got fired. It was the moment when I realised that no matter how hard I try, something needs to give. I can't be an assistant manager at my workplace and be a university student at the same time. The pace I was going at was not sustainable. It was the end of my second year, and I was exhausted, ready to give up and take a long holiday without books, articles, essays, and morning alarm clocks. But I had rent to cover, bills to pay, and lectures to attend. And most importantly, I had my vision and my classmates, who had become my friends.

"When life knocks you down, try to land on your back. Because if you can look up, you can get up. Let your reasons get you back up." Les Brown

I realised that I had built this image of Miss Independent, and I was so proud of doing it all by myself. Based on my previous heartbreak, I developed the following beliefs: I do not need anybody; If I let other people into my life, if I ask for help, I will be let down; I can't trust people; People will betray me; I can't be seen as vulnerable.

Well, let me just say that 'Miss Independent' was a mask I created, an illusion I was hiding behind, because, once again, I was crumbling inside. And after years of pretending to have everything under control and being the helper, I was the one who needed the help. I had to reorganise my priorities, let go of being a team lead at work, and shift my focus on what mattered most to me - completing my university degree and finding a new job with fewer responsibilities. Most importantly, I had to admit to my family and friends that I was fired from work. And ask for help.

"Some people believe holding on and hanging in there are signs of great strength. However, there are times when it takes much more strength to know when to let go and then do it." Ann Landers

To my surprise, once I admitted the fact I was struggling and started speaking about my challenges, the people around me resonated with me. Nobody criticised me, which was my biggest fear. Nobody said "Why don't you just give up? Why bother if you can't keep up?" But instead, we pulled together as a team and formed a study group. This was all so new to me! Back home, we students were always competing against each other; I was the brilliant one, always having all the answers, teacher's pet, as they say. And now, I was studying in a language that wasn't in my native tongue, living in a country far away from my family, and interacting with people in the same situation who wanted me to succeed. I was so grateful for overcoming my own pride and reaching out for help. Our collective struggle - we were all working in different full-time day jobs while studying - brought us closer together, and this study group stayed together until our graduation in July 2015.

"If you want to go fast, go by yourself. If you want to go far, go together." – African proverb

As for my MSc Occupational Psychology vision, I had found a workaround that I didn't realise was there until my last year. You see, the vision was not to be an Occupational Psychologist. The vision was to help companies and teams to improve and help people to have more job satisfaction, and I have found my own way of doing that. By working in an IT recruitment agency - yeah, I thought that I would be helping unemployed people find jobs. Hmm, that is not what recruitment is about. Recruitment is sales, headhunting and working for the commission, filling the roles for the client, and working for that shiny commission. You are awarded once you find the perfect candidate, and they accept the offer.

Because I had no idea what these people were actually doing, and I wanted to understand and have better conversations with them, I needed to learn a new language. I took the same principle in getting to the university with IELTS for my BSc. I bought Java for dummies and started reading it before my bedtime. The more I read, the more I wanted to know what exactly these people - my candidates - are working on. I became curious and started asking questions, being interested. After Java, which I didn't really enjoy as its database language and so-called back end, I started studying more visual interactive aspects of HTML, CSS, and JavaScript to have better conversations with my candidates. Long story short, I realised in the process that if any junior software developer can learn coding in their bedroom by simply following courses and practising, so can I. Once again, I was standing before this big question: What do I want?

Once my first agency announced redundancy plans, I decided to try my luck somewhere else, and I found a job as a talent manager in a new and promising space… which I walked away from in my very first week. It was a toxic place. I was working long hours, had to find new CVs for the next day in the evening after work, and still, nothing was good enough for the owner of the business. The first time I encountered him at my interview, something in me wasn't happy. That inner voice, which I shut down, was trying to tell me that he was not as lovely as he appeared, and I was soon to find that my intuition was right. This person who turned out to be my line manager was an amazing salesman, but his people skills were poor, to say the least. The whole office knew that, but as this guy was the owner of the company, he could pretty much do whatever he wanted in order to get his numbers, including shouting at his employees, and telling them that it's not a hard job, and how come I can't do it? I lasted four days in that place. On the fifth day, I got yet another phone call from my "manager" who was giving me very negative feedback; it was either walking away by myself, becoming ill from all the stress, or getting fired. I chose "the easy option" and packed my stuff. I still remember that feeling of joy, happiness, and freedom in my body when I shut the office door behind me. No, recruitment wasn't for me. That feeling of pure happiness, power, and pride that "I walked away for me" lasted only a few hours. Then, the fact of my new reality hit me like an anvil. I was unemployed and living in London, one of the most expensive places in the world, without a partner or the support of my family. And without a plan B. I was screwed... *What have I done?!*

Ask for what you want, not what you don't want.

I had to come to terms with changing my jobs and my career. Leaving the past recruiter version of me, which no longer served me in the process, and becoming unemployed. I spiralled into depression and was spending full days in my bed, not wanting to move, not eating properly, thinking about how much money I had left in my bank account, how much food I needed to eat in order to survive, and when the next bill was coming through, dreading that next bill coming through. It was a really dark place that I wouldn't wish on anyone.

Eventually, I got myself out of that funk by, once again, focusing on my vision: getting into IT. My job search was not leading anywhere. I didn't want to do recruitment anymore - it didn't resonate with me - but every single time I sent my CV for a recruitment job, I got a call-back. Yep, my CV was written with recruitment experience and was suitable only for recruitment jobs. It took a few dozen job applications to non-recruitment jobs without any response for me to realise that I needed help. I got my CV professionally rewritten for customer service roles, then registered at the local job centre for benefits because I needed some money to cover my rent and bills. At the job centre, I asked my adviser, Pauline (I still remember the name of this angel of a woman), for 'any IT courses they could send me for', thinking about doing something like learning Word or Excel. Anything to not sit at home on my butt and waste yet another day. And this lady handed me an opportunity that was not advertised anywhere around me, the opportunity I wouldn't get if I didn't ask – a Quality Assurance (QA) internship for graduates or career changers. Have you ever heard this phrase: *Ask, and it is given?* Well, this was exactly that. I asked and I was given the opportunity of a lifetime.

I have to say that my start in this internship role wasn't straightforward. I passed the interview and was told by the hiring person that we start in November, as they needed to fly a trainer from India to the UK. Then the start day got pushed from November to December. Then to January. So in December I was still unemployed, and when I visited my family for Christmas, my mum begged me to forget about this internship. My whole family was telling me it was a scam. *How do you know it will happen? They keep postponing, and you don't have anything solid, no contract, no set start date. Please, Blanka, go for the other 'normal job'* because I had an offer at another company to work as a bilingual customer service representative. Remember that CV that was rewritten by a professional? It worked.

So there I was, holding onto that vision of my first IT internship. It told me it would happen, while everyone around me was telling me otherwise. On top of this, I got scammed recently. In my effort to make some quick money, I signed up with a trading company and lost my investment. The company was not regulated, so even escalating the situation to the Financial Ombudsman didn't yield any results.

There were so many questions on my mind: Who do I trust? My family or my own inner knowledge? But when I did that before, I got myself in trouble. Do you remember that second recruitment job and trading company? Those were both my independent decisions. What if my family knows better than I do? Eventually, I got tired of constantly explaining that it would work! I started doubting my vision of the IT internship and signed a contract with the other company.

Where attention goes, energy flows.

Once again, the Universe showed me that this is not the right path for me. In my first two weeks in this new role, I had so many technical issues that I was not even able to access the system. Apparently, there was an issue with one of my entrance exam test results which were part of the hiring process. My results went missing. Yep, I was not supposed to be working for this company as I literally didn't exist in the system, and I was asked to redo the test, which I passed. However, I had to wait for a whole week for my details to be updated in the system. I couldn't do my job properly, and I felt like an out-of-place fraud. Hopeless and helpless, because I could only wait for this issue to be resolved by managers. So, as you can imagine, when the IT internship program called me during this "I can't work here" situation and asked me if I was still interested, I used the system malfunction as my way out and quit.

The following week, I started the IT internship, which was supposed to be a scam. I remember walking down to the office based in Marble Arch, listening to Jim Rohn's "The Day That Changed My Life" audio recording, getting inspired, and thinking if other people can change their lives by the power of belief, so can I. It didn't matter that I didn't study computer science. Only one member of our group did, as I learned while making friends with my fellow trainees. I immersed myself in studying the software testing subject, determined to pass my exams, and after a few months of training from 0 to QA Engineer, there was the final hurdle – an interview with hiring managers. This was it, the point in my life when my seniors in the industry would decide if I was ready to be an "IT person."

I brought my best to that interview, all my passion, determination, and skills. I was so impressed that the head of the QA team was a lady, and I loved her from the very first time we got introduced and shook hands. I knew, at that moment, that the QA team was the place for me, that I wanted to be like her. Mel was and still is my role model. I wanted to be on her team, learn from her, and become like her, and I was accepted for my internship on the client's side.

Once again, the universe wanted to teach me a lesson, because my first QA project was on - a drum roll, please - Global Regulations. I kid you not. I had to learn different regulatory reporting systems for different transaction types and global regions. I finally understood where I went wrong with the trading company. Let's just say that they were based outside the regulatory grid and were not supposed to do business in the UK. But when you are desperate for money, you let your guard down, and these people can target you and use you for their profit. The lesson here: always read the fine print before you sign. No matter what. You can thank me later.

    Five years later, we have come full circle, because today, once again, I'm working as the Team Lead, not in a coffee shop but in an IT consultancy. I'm also a founder of BeFreeWithBlanka, where I facilitate transformational sessions for women who had enough of the same old in finding that vision and rediscovering their voices and their power. I'm helping my employer by encouraging my fellow team members to speak up, and I'm debugging software and human minds. Somehow it all came together in a completely different form than what I thought.

    "The How is not your responsibility." – Amanda Frances

Here's the thing: you don't need to know how you will get there in order to achieve your goals and your vision. I thought I needed to be an Occupational Psychologist in order to help others. Instead, I had to go on my own personal healing journey to peel those layers and heal the old emotional wounds. And find NLP and RTT as a client.

I thought that I needed to fix people by knowing more to save them from.. themselves, I guess? Well, here's the truth: we can't change or save others. We can only change ourselves and guide others on their own transformational journey.

I thought I needed someone who knew stuff to show me how to live my life. I was afraid to make mistakes. Today I'm welcoming challenges and living my life on my terms. And finally, after so many years of hating my surname – *Why do you call me by that name? Did I do something wrong?* – I'm embracing my family name of *Volna*; in Czech, it literally means "be free." I'm holding onto my vision of healing the world, one woman at a time. Healing without medications by giving people back their power and their voice and rebuilding the trust in their own intuition.

Because at the end of the day, if we keep giving our power away and blaming other people, who are we hurting? Only ourselves. So, I encourage you to hold onto that vision, see it in bright colours, hear what you hear, and feel what you feel. Right now, in your body. Because, my friend, the mind doesn't know the difference between reality and imagination.

I will leave you with this:

You can create your vision and your future by focusing on what you want, believing you can have it, and if people tell you otherwise, well, thank them for their feedback but keep focus on that vision. You can do it, you are enough, and you are worth it.

Go for your dreams, trust in yourself, your calling, and the universe, which always has your back. And leave the how to figure itself out; it's not your responsibility.

> You got this!
>
> Lots of love and healing light,

Chapter Seven

BREAKING WALLS- FINDING MY WORTH

By Thelma Birchall

Preface

Sylvia mentioned this project to me because she knows a lot about me. She believed I should be a part of this project, which I initially contested. I have life stories, but I never thought of myself as a writer.

I was apprehensive about putting my story out there. I had all these negative thoughts flooding my mind. I thought it would be boring to sit down and write about myself and my life. I thought my story wasn't interesting enough, and that nobody would want to read it. I went on with this negative self-talk for a good long while. What if people think it's rubbish? Who would want to know about me?

Nevertheless, looking back, I remember how I once jokingly said to Sylvia that my life is literally a book full of diverse stories, and that I could write a book about them. She definitely took me up on my word, and here I am today. Why did I say that?

Even though I have never written a book, I knew I would not like writing. It would just be an added chore on top of all the other numerous chores I have.

When I was considering it, I thought I have had so much drama in my life, but I keep on fighting. Maybe I could talk about these experiences. I know there are people who are facing challenges out there, and struggling to find a way to cope, needing a way out of their struggles.

When I finally decided to participate, I thought that this could help someone to not give up so easily in life. Okay. I will write something. But what? Which part of my crazy life do I write about? You will find out in this story about me.

I hope this helps at least one person who has been in similar situations to mine.

Well, here goes…

The Walls in My Life

Growing up, I lived a comfortable life and did not have to do much. I was mostly lazy and could not be bothered; I did not see why I had to think about the future. All I had to do was to enjoy my current life which was provided to me by my generous parents. Ah, my parents. They were both busy working, but they were so generous and loving. My parents were comfortable, money-wise, but I would not say that they were rich. They had their issues, but they were good people.

Nevertheless, ever since I was little, I have always been told that I was vague and confusing by other people. What do they know about me? I was told that I was lazy and did not seem to care about my education. Even though these words bothered me, I acted as though I did not care. Maybe they were right? I did not care that much about learning, or maybe I did. I did care if I had bad grades, and I did care when my parents were unimpressed by my not-so-good grades. But that was when I did not put in the time at school. It was too much effort to do extra studies. Why did I have to write exams? I would often ask. It was so boring. Don't get me wrong. When I made an effort, I was great. But I did not have the best grades in school because I never tried. I had to do extra courses to get into college, and I completed college with two babies. I was not satisfied. I wanted more. I wanted to prove that I was a somebody.

I just wanted to be happy. Don't we all? My idea of happiness was never doing extra work or extra studying to make other people happy. I was stubborn and strong-willed, but unhappy with other people and their thoughts, ideas, and words about me. How dare they judge me in that manner? Who do they think they are? I often found myself asking.

The big question was: how can I be happy when I have always been told that I will not amount to much? That I will never be able to go to university? That I'm not clever enough to do so? I was also told it would be impossible to go to university with two babies. What was

I thinking, leaving my precious babies at home, and going off to study? Am I a bad mum?

The other question was: did I want to go to university because I wanted to, or because I wanted to show these horrible judgemental people that they were so wrong about me? Do I really care what people think about me? Am I that petty? Maybe a little. Ah, there we go getting drawn into these negative thoughts again.

I lost myself and my way at a very young age, doubting my abilities and deciding that I wasn't good enough. I let other people's judgement of me cloud my judgement of myself. See, it's so easy to be swayed into negative thoughts when all you see is a negative understanding of yourself. It took me a while to mentally set myself a challenge, to go on a journey to find my self-worth. If that's what they think, I will show them one day.

The Diagnosis:

I went to university for a couple of years, doing something I did not quite enjoy. I struggled with certain aspects of the course, and I needed to find out why. I applied to have an assessment done, and was diagnosed with 'slight dyslexia', and now I had a label. I cried for a whole day. Why me? I was forgetful, lazy, and did not enjoy studying, but I was quite clever when I made the effort. What did "slight dyslexia" even mean? Either you have dyslexia, or you don't, right? I might not have been great at maths, but I did not have dyslexia. I knew I was clever if I made the right effort. I was tired and hadn't slept properly the night before the assessment. That could have been the reason, right?

Anyway, I still had the label. I just wanted to scream, "Why does everything have to be so difficult? Why me? How dare you put a label on me. I'm amazing! Don't be putting your labels on me."

Being diagnosed broke me. I did not want a label, even though I wanted to understand why I previously struggled with two subjects and my degree. Maybe I should not argue so much and agree with and accept what they tell me. That will make everything so much easier.

I continued with my course, but my diagnosis weighed heavily on me. In the second year, I found out I was pregnant with my third child. I was ill most of the time but kept going to lessons because I didn't want to become a "disappointment." I had placement two weeks after I had my third baby, which was hard. I had sleepless nights, I was tired, and had pains, but kept on going to placement and preparing for exams. I was also unfortunately assigned a supervisor who did not like me and found faults with everything I did. I had enough and gave up. After all, I had always been told I was not good enough and never would be, so why fight it? Is this truly me? Will I not amount to much?

I left the course, and there were so many unhappy feelings, while I still had a baby and two toddlers to care for. I talked to people who I thought were my friends, looking for support and acceptance. Instead, I just got a judging look, as though I was missing a part of me. As if I was incomplete. I lost friendships, and that broke me a little. I was sad, but I had to find a way to cope. I knew if people couldn't accept me for who I was, then they were not my people. I learned to let go of those people.

However, I was not all alone. I still had my family and friends who didn't think any differently of me. I was still the same person to them, and they loved me for it.

I decided to forget about it all and get on with my family life. However, I still couldn't shake the label off. I couldn't let myself be a failure. Was dyslexia the reason I had made so many poor choices in life? I have three young babies with no degree. Maybe I did this all wrong. Maybe I should have fought to get my degree before getting married and having kids. The normal way! But I love my husband, and I love my kids. They are my life. How can they be wrong? No, how can you even think like that, Thelma? Don't be silly. They are the reason why you are here today, the reason why you don't give up, the reason you will push on. You will find a way, you always do.

Well, it is time to learn and grow, right? But why do I have to do what society tells me to do in order to be happy? Why do I feel like I'm not good enough? What is my worth?

I felt useless, I felt lost, and I felt disappointed in myself. I couldn't let myself down again. My family has always been my comfort and has been there to keep me sane. Mum asked me to pray. She always asks me to pray about everything. The problem is, why do I keep facing trials and tribulations? Maybe God has a purpose for me, but what is it? Whatever it is, I wouldn't mind it being a mansion with lots of money that I wouldn't know what to do with. Well, maybe give some to the people I love, and maybe give some to charity. All of that would be nice, but not realistic. Not right now, anyway.

Breaking the Walls and Finding My Worth

I still had the problems I had to deal with first, so I went on my knees and prayed. I asked God through my tears for help. You see, I was brought up as a Christian but had lost my faith along the way. He answered me with a superhero friend who came out of nowhere to help me. A friend (perhaps a guardian angel?) who I hadn't spoken to for a good while. She listened to me, then went away and researched before coming back to me. She told me all is not lost and showed me opportunities out there that I never thought were possible. When I needed help, God sent her.

I believe I am blessed because I have such strong and amazing females in my family (mum and two sisters) who always stand by me, advise and support me no matter what. They are probably my guardian angels too, because I do not know where I will be without their caring words, support, kindness, honesty, and kick in the bum when needed.

These amazing people guide me and help me readjust and set me back to restart mode so I can sort my head out and move out of the darkness (sadness) and into the light (positivity and motivational zone).

Dr Sylvia Forchap-Likambi et al

The Power of Choice:

Whenever we encounter life challenges and sometimes feel defeated and lost in life, we are always presented with two fundamental choices: do nothing and live in regret or fight for what you want. I knew which choice I was going for.

I applied for an undergraduate degree in health, and I was accepted. There were still people discouraging me, saying that it would be useless to go to university with three babies. I knew it was going to be difficult, going to university with three babies. Again, I was reminded that it would be difficult, impossible.

Well, they were right about it being difficult, challenging even, but not impossible. I just had to work harder and plan more efficiently, studying at night while people slept or staying at home when people went out to have fun. I focussed on going to university and completing my course, and nothing was going to stop me. Maybe I was not being the greatest mum, leaving those poor babies behind to go to university, but I was doing it for them too. That cannot be a bad thing, right? So, I went ahead and started the new program at university.

One day, in one of my lessons with the lead lecturer – the one who accepted me into the course – he made a spelling mistake while writing something down. I noticed it straight away, but I said nothing, and nobody else corrected him. He noticed his mistake and apologised, saying he was dyslexic. What? A university lecturer was dyslexic? I respected him so much, and he had the same condition I had. But he is so intelligent, he leads the program, how on earth can he have the same condition? I arranged to have a meeting with him and managed to find out more about his dyslexia. I mentioned my fear of my dyslexia affecting my course. He said that if he can do it, I can too.

Yes, it was true. Very true. He showed me a few strategies he used. My problem was not the same as his, as I had a problem with memory, and had to reread things for them to stick in my head. I knew how to cope with my problem, so why was I getting worried? How do I let a word such as "dyslexia" take control of my thought process? I am in control of who I am, and I can complete university. I can do this. I continued with my program, while working with three children. University, run home, and go to work. It was difficult, but I was determined to finish university, and I did. Successfully.

I even went on to apply for a master's degree afterwards and completed that too. I am unbreakable. I had found my power, and I found I did not have to fight myself anymore. I just had to accept who I was and work hard to cross every obstacle in my way. I understood that if God had given me another shot at getting my undergraduate degree, then it was meant to be.

I now had qualifications, but I did not yet feel successful. I wanted more. I went off to work; some jobs I enjoyed, and others not so much. I was still lost and looking for my worth. Trapped, suffocating, and not knowing what I want and who I am anymore. I struggled to cope with some jobs and certain people I came across, but I enjoyed other jobs and got on well with other people. I guess that is just part of life, right?

I had a lot of life experiences. I met new people, I lost people. Opportunities, disappointments, happiness, sadness, and in it all, I had still not found my worth. I might not have been rich, but I had a family, love, education, and work, but I was still lost. Where was my worth?

Dyslexia occasionally will creep up on me again. I thought I had broken those barriers, I thought I was over all of that. I was to an extent, but I was still aware it was there. I wished I was not dyslexic. Why was I letting one word affect me again? I questioned myself. I knew I could fight through my troubles, but do I always have to? What was my worth again? Will I have to break these barriers forever? How much fight do I have left within me?

Simple answer: a whole lot more.

Punch, crash, kick! I will keep fighting for my worth. What is it, anyway? Will I ever find it? Does it matter if I find it?

Society tells us to be worthy, respected, and important. Stuff society. Don't get me wrong, I would love an easy life, but an easy life does not seem to love me. I do not like barriers and challenges. I do like breaking them, though. How long will it take me to find this life of luxury? This easy worry-free life?

Finding My Worth

I recently had my fourth baby. I have four beautiful children and a supporting husband. Oh, my dear husband, what a strong and amazing man for having to listen to me complain and go through my troubles. How does he do it? Looking at my kids, intelligent, happy, gorgeous, loving, and kind, I feel lucky to be their mummy. I am everything to them.

Hey, I haven't done too bad at all.

I am their protector. I am happy to be their personal cook, driver, adviser, carer, and servant, but most of all, I am their mum and they love me, and I love them too. They do not care if I am perfect or not, so why do I feel like I am not enough? Watching their beautiful faces and hearing them tell me they love me shows me that I am everything to them. They are everything to me. I know I am worthy of my wonderful family. That is one. I have qualifications. That is two.

But there is still something missing, and I still need to find it. However, I now know I can find it and complete that challenge with the right tools. I will always have new goals, and they may come with challenges, but I have a new understanding now. I understand I can achieve anything and everything I set my mind to, with the right tools and the right people, and that I am worthy of doing so. It has taken me many years to understand that I am worthy of anything I want to be worthy of. I am in control of myself and my thoughts.

Thank goodness for that, because this acceptance of who I am gave me the confidence to go back and relearn dyslexia; it is simply a "struggle with words."

Hey, that is what I have. Sometimes I struggle to find the right words and names in a conversation which I used to find embarrassing but I have learnt that I am not the only one who struggles with this. My writing skills may not be perfect, but I have ways to improve.

The main problem was assuming this condition made me less of a human than I am. It was flawed and I vigorously believed that, which stopped me from doing so much more for myself. I let my mind believe the untruth because I assumed the condition caused more defects, which I could possibly have but did not have.

Am I glad I have gotten over that?

Yes, yes, yes. I certainly am.

Guess what, forgetting words does not make me less of who I am. I am still an intelligent, kind, honest, loving, caring, passionate, and friendly person who is still full of mischief. I am not perfect, but that is okay. This is who I am and that is okay.

I have had struggles and I have listened to the wrong people. I have learnt from them. I will have more letdowns and disappointments. It is jolly good that I am experienced in these fields and have my own personal ammunition to deal with them. What is life without drama anyway? It will be pretty boring. Right?

I will break these barriers when I get to them in my own time. I know I had to learn through all my trials and tribulations to be a better version of myself. It has been a tough but rewarding journey. I have wasted time worrying about things I never should have, but I am here, and I am a survivor and even more, a victor. I have come to the realisation that sometimes failure is needed to push your way forward to success, as long as you do not let it break and destroy you or give

Visionary Woman

up and quit. Just like you do not let success get to your head. It's important to have that balance and remain humble. Some of the worst challenges I have had to overcome were with my own inner thoughts, limiting beliefs, and judgements of myself. I was so unkind to myself. I'm glad I managed to get through those challenging times. If you are currently reading this and you are at the stage or point in your life, I want you to know that you too can overcome these inner hurdles. You have to commit to be kinder and more loving towards yourself— showing more compassion towards yourself.

I am blessed to have great friends and family, even after shedding those who were in the way of my progress. I am blessed to have people to turn to if I'm having a bad day. Those strong support systems are a necessity to have. It is often said, your network determines your net worth, and this truly resonates with me. Surround yourself with the people who are genuinely happy to see you grow, to see you thrive, and who actually encourage you to do so.

I know who I am now. I am a strong, resilient, ambitious, adaptive, loving, and visionary woman. I'm amazing. I have everything I need and deserve everything I have. I am worthy because I am more than enough.

Do I have regrets? No. I had to experience everything to know my worth. I am unique, and I accept myself. I might be a late bloomer, but I am happy and I love myself. I don't have anything to prove to anybody. I continue to fight my battles and will fight any other battles I have along the way. But guess what? I have the ammunition to fight. I am at peace with who I am. I am enough, and that is my worth.

Guess what, if I can find mine, then you can too. It is never too late to find your worth. You are enough.

Words of Wisdom

- Embracing the storms with optimism

You will face defeat and challenges, but never stay defeated. As the saying goes, nothing is permanent. Not even the hard times. Accept that change happens, and then let it take its course, as terrifying as it may seem. It always comes to pass. Storms never last forever.

I faced challenges that were obstacles designed to develop me into a character strong enough to face other challenges I came across. Stronger, more confident. These are the life changes I needed to survive and overcome this crazy world.

As humans, we spend so much time in life focusing on the bad things that happen to us and completely forget about the many good things in our lives.

Why do we do this? Work on the positives and enjoy your life.

So, I occasionally struggle with words, so what? Well, guess what? I broke my barrier. How? I went ahead to work in a career that involved talking to people.

Visionary Woman

I am a nutritionist and a health coach. I guess the best way to silence your critics is by doing what they say you can't do, right? Break those barriers.

- Overcoming Fear:

Looking back, it was never just about finding my worth, because I am worth so much more than I ever gave myself credit for. It was my fears; fears of losing, fears of not being good enough, fears of not being successful, fears of being dyslexic. For a good while, I let those fears stop me from fighting and moving on to great things.

Once we stop fearing what will be and accept who we are, it is easy to refocus and break those barriers, those worries that have been eating us alive for so long. We must make peace with who we are and accept and value ourselves just as we are. We cannot please everyone or meet everyone's expectations about us. Hence, we must learn to let go of every fear of rejection, disapproval, judgement, etc. It is vital that we know our worth and never allow anyone or condition to determine what we are worth. I would like you to affirm these words with me:

I am an achiever.

I am unstoppable.

I am worthy, every bit of me.

I am courageous and fearless.

I am blessed.

We must remain grateful at all times and recognise our blessings. We should never stop counting our blessings and proclaiming we are blessed. It is fundamental that we continually examine our core beliefs and cultivate positive, empowering beliefs that enable us to face fear and overcome it. Focusing on our strengths, abilities, and surrounding ourselves with a great army of amazing and inspiring people will go a long way in building our confidence and courage.

Our world needs us to show up every single day and be authentically and unapologetically us; unique as we serve in our greatest calling and full potential!

Watch out world. Here I come.

Chapter Eight

VICTORY AT LAST

By Ellen Mandizvidza

Preface

When I was first approached by Dr. Sylvia to be a part of this project, I thought to myself, I don't really have anything to write about or share with the world. I never thought I had a story. But when I spoke with her and took her through my story in-depth, she was left gobsmacked and told me I had a truly inspiring story to share with the world. She said it represented the epitome of hope, restoration, and victory for many. She jokingly added that my life is a complete package; I represent hope, rebirth, restoration, victory, a new beginning, you name it…

Now I can only hope that my story inspires, encourages, and strengthens someone who is going through a difficult time.

My Life History

My life hasn't been all that great, to be perfectly honest. It was a painful, traumatic, and sad one, but I thank God for allowing me to walk through that path. These traumas happened for me, not to me. My dad passed away when I was nine years old, and after his funeral, my mum went back to live with her family. I grew up overnight from being Mum and Dad's princess to a maid, gardener, babysitter, cook, and cleaner. I switched from doing chores that are suitable for a nine-year-old child to work that is suitable for adults.

After Dad's death I lived with my aunt and uncle. My aunt was not very kind to me. The only day that she did not ask me to remove my clothes and hit me was when my uncle - her husband - had come back from the city where he worked.

Going to school was a dream for me. I would go to school once every two weeks or once a month. Before going to school, I had to do all of the household chores first, including fetching water from the borehole. After school I was supposed to fetch firewood and cook the evening meal for the entire family. The very year that my father died, I started to cook "sadza" (a thick porridge made from maize flour) for nine people. It was not easy because the pot was too big for me, and I sustained burns on my wrists. I have a permanent scar from those burns. If I didn't cook sadza well, my aunt would ask me to eat all the sadza without relish. From the day I stayed with my aunt, I never played with other kids. If she asked me to go somewhere, she used to spit on the ground and I was supposed to come back before the saliva dried up; if I failed to do that, she would hit me bare skinned, as usual. I remember one day she hit me on the head with a bottle and I bled. The following day I went to school and the teacher asked me what had happened, as I had some blood on my hair. I told him that my aunt hit me with a bottle when I went back home. My aunt was told that I told the teacher about the incident, and she hit me as usual. She then asked me to go and tell the teacher that I had lied to him, and that I was pricked by barbed wire. After telling the teacher her narrative, which was obviously a lie, the teacher also hit me.

I endured neglect alongside physical, emotional, verbal, and psychological abuse. One day I was sick and tired of being beaten by my aunt, so I ran away and slept in the bush. Regardless of going to school on rare occasions, I wrote my grade 7 examinations in the last year of primary school and passed, but unfortunately, there was no money for me to go to high school, even though my guardians got all of my dad's pension. The headmaster pleaded with my aunt to send me to high school to no avail. Instead of going to high school, I repeated grade 7. The previous year, my mum had come to take us so that we could go with her to the city, but my aunt and uncle were not there so she left us.

The year that I repeated my grade 7, my mum returned to take us; we went to live with her and although she was very poor, she loved us dearly and would do whatever it took for us to be happy. My mum was poor. Even though she worked, her salary was meagre, and it was not enough to pay for our basic needs. We often went to bed without food. When the time came for me to write my GCSE, my mum did not have any money for the examination fee, so she had to borrow some money from a friend. I failed my GCSE that year, but thanks to my uncle who paid my fees, I was able to retake the subjects I had failed.

Several years went by and I eventually got married and became pregnant with my first child. As if life hadn't had enough of me, I lost my first baby and I did not take this very well. I remember hitting and biting the hospital staff after the death of my child. After the loss, I was very ill for six months and almost lost my life. I vowed to never have a child again. My in-laws sent me back to my mum's, saying they had given up on me. After returning to my mum's, I never saw any of my in-laws again, even though they lived only 20 minutes' walk away from my mum's. During this difficult period, my husband was the only one visiting, while his family only started visiting after six months.

As they say, time heals all wounds. Indeed, after some time I tried for a baby again, and God blessed me with a baby boy. Two years later, I got pregnant again; but unfortunately, it ended in a miscarriage. It was very challenging, but I am grateful to God for stretching forth His righteous hand and healing me. I got pregnant again in 2012; it was another difficult pregnancy, far worse than the previous. Three months into my pregnancy, I felt so ill that I was unable to work until my baby was born. I would literally crawl up and down the stairs in order to access any bedroom in my home. On this particular day, while I was cooking, l collapsed and was rushed into hospital where I was admitted for several days and diagnosed with gallstones.

When it rains it pours. My husband, who has always been well with no medical conditions, collapsed out of the blue one day and ended up having head surgery; another challenging experience for us.

Living in England, we couldn't afford the cost of maids to help with household chores, considering that we also had a five-year child at home. At the time, even though we both worked for a private company, we were unpaid while off sick. We are profoundly grateful to the Zimbabwean community and our church, who stood by us during these challenging times. Some prayed, others helped with household chores, while some even offered financial support.

After a very challenging pregnancy, I finally had a bouncing baby boy, though I left with some complex health issues. In January 2014, when my baby was less than a year old, I then had surgery to remove the gallstones.

A month later, while still on maternity leave and recovering from surgery, I launched my first business, a recruitment agency (a vision I conceived in 2005 but wasn't motivated to make a reality, because I had a job and was financially comfortable). Left without an income, the pain of being financially broke drove me to launch the business.

In 2016, I was very ill again, which heavily affected my business. This time, I was admitted to an oncology ward since the doctors suspected that I had cancer. It was heart-breaking seeing people who were in pain due to cancer. In 2017, I was diagnosed with a meningioma, and a year later (2018) I got diagnosed with a blocked kidney. Within a few months of the diagnosis, both kidneys were blocked, and I had stents inserted. In 2018 alone, I had surgery under general anaesthesia four times.

Now, you would think with everything I have gone through and am still going through, I would be broken, knocked down, resentful, with all sorts of mental health problems, and asking "Why me?" Nonetheless, this is not the case. In fact, it was never an option! I still have the drive to live, to be healed, and be financially free to support my family and ensure that my children or any other child out there never goes through what I went through in my childhood or allow their circumstances and health conditions to define and limit them from living a life of purpose and impact. Above all, I made the choice to use my journey as a message of hope and inspiration to women and mothers out there who are hurting or in pain. I chose to rise beyond my challenges… to thrive beyond my sight!

Now, how do you thrive beyond the endless challenges thrown at you or that life presents to you? Using my own personal experience, I would like to share the following with you and hope that you, too, are inspired to thrive and look beyond your current challenges or circumstances.

Thriving Beyond Challenges

"My mission in life is not merely to survive, but to thrive, and to do so with some passion, some compassion, some humour and some style," Maya Angelou

For me to thrive beyond challenges, I had to become self-aware, which involved becoming aware of who I am, where I was, what was holding me back, what I was capable of achieving, and who I wanted to be.

Visionary Woman

In life there are things you can control and things you can't. I had no choice on who was going to look after me and take care of me after the death of my father. I also had no choice on what challenges or health conditions could affect me or my husband. These incidents were completely out of my control and were never my decision. Notwithstanding, I had the power to choose how I responded to everything that has happened to me to date, which could either be to dwell on my past or to move on and embrace the future and endless opportunities ahead of me. I choose the latter and decided to take full responsibility over my life. I am conscious of the fact I am the director and CEO of my life. Hence, it was up to me to survive or thrive beyond barriers. I made a conscious decision and I was so intentional about it so I could thrive beyond my challenges and every barrier I encountered.

Consequently, to thrive beyond the barriers of life we need to exhibit the following traits and qualities:

Gratitude

"Gratitude unlocks the fullness of life. It turns what we have into enough, and more. It turns denial into acceptance, chaos to order, confusion to clarity. It can turn a meal into a feast, a house into a home, a stranger into a friend.

Gratitude makes sense of our past, brings peace for today, and creates a vision for tomorrow," Melody Beattie.

I am profoundly grateful to God for allowing me to walk through this difficult journey, although I don't wish it on anyone. I think I was the perfect person to have walked through it. I had to make a choice whether I should continue to suffer by blaming people or God for what I went through. The day I decided to trade expectation for appreciation, I became liberated, I was able to thrive because I let go of blame and questioning why it happened to me. When I look to where I was and where I am now, I have every reason to thank God. Gratitude is the key principle to our success. It helps people to feel more positive emotions, relish good experiences, improve their health, deal with adversity, and build strong relationships.

Being Prayerful:

Prayer helped me to see beyond my problems and take the focus off the mountains and challenges I was faced with and looked within, to God, my source of strength and hope. With prayer, I was able to hold it together and to have peace in the storm. Philippians 4:6-7. It enabled me to put my trust in Jesus, the author and finisher of our faith. Hebrews 12:2

Cast all your anxiety on Him because He cares for you. 1 Peter 5:7

As human beings we cannot do without our creator and higher power. We should have communion with God, our source of everything.

In a nutshell, prayer helps us to love unconditionally and forgive those who have hurt us. We need the grace of God for us to handle setbacks without stumbling.

Self-love

"Friendship with oneself is all-important, because without it one cannot be friends with anyone else in the world," Eleanor Roosevelt

"Don't forget to tell yourself positive things daily. You must love yourself internally for you to glow externally," Hannah Bronfman

I had to love myself first as I can't give what I don't have. Loving myself helped me feel happier, more positive, take better care of myself, have self-confidence, self-worth, and improve my self-esteem. Self-love made me fearless and at peace with myself. There is no shame in being your biggest fan and personal cheerleader to get you pumped up to tackle the world. Hence, in your darkest hours, always remember to love yourself and be your number-one ally.

Forgiveness

"It's one of the greatest gifts you can give yourself, to forgive. Forgive everybody," Maya Angelou

"The weak can never forgive. Forgiveness is an attribute of the strong," Mahatma Gandhi

Even though my past was so traumatic, for my healing to be complete I had to make a conscious, deliberate decision to release feelings of resentment and unforgiveness towards the people who had hurt me, regardless of whether they deserved it or not. Resentment always hurts you more than it does the person you resent. I forgave but did not forget. Forgiveness helps us to have peace of mind, it frees us from bitterness, and empowers us to recognise the pain we experience without letting that pain define who we are, which in turn enables us to heal and move on with our lives.

Love

"You never lose by loving. You always lose by holding back," Barbara De Angellis

"Be the love you never received," Rune Lazuli

Regardless of how I was treated, I chose to let love prevail. After all, love conquers all. I had to love everyone unconditionally. I believe it was not my aunt's fault; maybe she had not received love (you can't give what you don't have) or she had unresolved past hurts. Hurting people easily hurt others. Love is not simply an emotion or feeling, but it is an action. For example, when my uncle was unable to pay school fees for his young children, he used to ask me, and I would give him. The very person who said there was no money for me to go to high school, even though he was getting our father's pension. I decided to look for my cousins as we were not in contact; I found them, and we are on good terms.

Letting go of the past

"We are products of our past but we don't have to be prisoners of it," – Rick Warren

"Consider that the path you were once on was meant to end when it did. Obsessing about plans lost or changed is a barrier to holistic wealth because it keeps you stuck in the past unable to move forward," Keisha Blair

Visionary Woman

I refused to let any negative situation that I went through define me and I refused to be held back by my past. I believe it was a place for learning and not living. I had no control over my past, but I had the power to change my future. I can't live beyond barriers when I am carrying baggage and living in my past. I became familiar and comfortable with my past. I felt I had to let go and get out of my comfort zone for me to thrive. Holding on to your past eats your life away; you can't change your past, none of it. Make peace with this truth and move on.

Focusing on the present and future

"Where focus goes energy flows," Tony Robbins

I had to focus on what I could control, which is my present and my future. Where focus goes, energy follows. If I continued to focus on what I went through, I'd continue to suffer, as suffering leads to more suffering. We must choose to expand and intensify our focus on our present and future, to give power and life to our present and future.

Seeing beauty in the bad

"Everything has beauty but not everyone sees it," Confucius

There can be beauty in the bad moments if we are willing to see it. The beauty in my bad experiences doesn't take away the bad, but I had to take the opportunity to learn, change, and grow from it. Out of my pain came goodness, and it fuels me to do what I do. You must always stay optimistic and hopeful, understanding that all bad moments provide us with opportunities, such as:

a) Growth

Hard times help us grow if we let them, and they build our character. The hard times I have experienced in my life have helped me grow to be a better person.

b) Life Lessons

Bad times always come with a lesson or many lessons. I looked for the lessons and learnt from them. I hereby encourage you to look for lessons in every challenging situation. I guarantee you that if we look long enough or deeper into the bad times, we would always find lessons or treasures to take along with us and improve our lives. I also came to the understanding that bad times are often life tests not designed to destroy, and once overcome, enable us to move on to the next level of our growth and success.

c) Change

Human beings don't want change if things are good. We remain stagnant if we continue in our comfortable and familiar situation. But if we are put under pressure and hardship, we are moulded into something new and possibly better than we could have ever imagined.

Due to what I went through, one of my highest values is contribution. I pay school fees for people who are in need and contribute financially to widows. I feel for people who are struggling. Out of my pain came goodness. It has fuelled me to do the work I now do.

Building Courage and Trust

"Courage is the most important of all the virtues because without courage, you can't practice any other virtue consistently," Maya Angelou

"Love cannot live where there is no trust," Edith Hamilton

The person I looked up to and who I was supposed to trust abused me. As a result, I found it very difficult to trust people and to believe in them. I was suspicious of people's intentions and motivations, and I struggled to form healthy and stable relationships with other people. I had to learn to trust myself first before I could trust others. Due to what I went through I also always anticipated pain. I found it difficult to act because of fear. I am convicted that for us to thrive beyond our past pain and challenges, we must learn to use fear as power and energy to act. I did not fight fear, but I had to dance with fear and to act in spite of fear. I learned to have courage in the face of fear.

Harnessing The Power of Thoughts

"A man is but the product of his thoughts what he thinks, he becomes," Mahatma Gandhi

"Your thoughts are the architects of your destiny," David O McKay

For me to thrive I had to change my mindset and deal with the root causes of my problems. What is underground creates what is above the ground. I had to do great inner work on the power of my thinking for me to thrive beyond barriers. My greatest power is my ability to choose my own thoughts and to conquer the negative ones. I had to change my mindset from that of an abused child to the person God sees and calls me to be. As a man thinketh so is he. I refused to let the negative situation I had gone through affect me, so I rose above my negative mindset. While we cannot control our outer world, we must always take full responsibility for controlling our inner world. Beliefs can create or destroy us, so we must learn to replace every disempowering belief with empowering beliefs.

After the loss of my son, I became very ill. Most people thought that I was not going to make it. Looking at my mum and siblings, my heart broke. Their financial situation had already changed for the worse as their breadwinner was lying on her deathbed, and she had not had an income for a while. I made a conscious decision not to continue lying on my deathbed. I was so intentional about it; I prayed for God to give me another chance to live, and I refused to think about myself and to look at my situation. I was determined to go back to work and ensure that none of my siblings will ever go to bed on an empty stomach again. I cried to God not to let history repeat itself; my mum struggled to raise the examination fee needed for me to take my GSCE, and that was not going to happen to any of my siblings.

My mindset was set on life and victory, and I ensured that at every given moment, my thoughts were in alignment with this mindset. That drove me to rise up from my deathbed. I knew I was definitely a victor and not a victim and had the power to change my situation with God's grace, which propelled me to go back to work again.

Being Confident

"Self-confidence is a superpower. Once you start to believe in yourself, magic starts happening," Unknown

What I went through caused me to constantly doubt myself. I lost confidence and had low self-esteem. I refuse to let these things continue to haunt me. Instead of this, I chose to embrace my true self. I became accustomed to being authentically raw.

My past made me feel worthless, and I was unable to differentiate between what was good and bad in me. When I thought I had done a good thing, my aunt would say it was wrong and beat me up. Before my aunt, everything I did was never good. That's why she would beat me every day. Being unable to differentiate between good and bad in my everyday life caused me to live a confused life. I had to believe in myself and my ability to make good decisions. I had to trust my judgement and not allow other people's opinions about me determine who I was or was becoming.

It is fundamental for us to understand who we truly are, the good intentions and kindness within us, in order to know our worth and be able to trust ourselves more.

Positive Relationships

"Human connection is the most vital aspect of our existence, without the sweet touch of another being we are lonely stars in an empty space waiting to shiny gloriously," Joe Straynge

"There is simply no pill that can replace human connection. There is no pharmacy that can fill the need for compassionate interaction with others. There is no panacea. The answer to human suffering is both within us and between us," Dr Joanne Cacciatore

Human beings are profoundly social creatures. One of our greatest desires is to be loved and belong. As humans, we crave contact and connection with other people. Maslow's hierarchy of needs includes a sense of belonging as a major need that motivates human behaviour, just like food, shelter, and safety.

I appreciate God for blessing me with an amazing family and friends who supported and cared for me when I was going through hardships. Positive, healthy connections helped me to feel happier, healthier, and fulfilled. Connecting with other human beings has a positive impact on our health and well-being. A landmark study showed that a lack of social connection is a greater detriment to health than obesity, smoking, and high blood pressure.

You don't have to be on your own when you are going through a difficult time. Asking for help is not a weakness but a virtue. Most of us don't have it altogether, pretending to be okay doesn't do any of us any good. Knowing that you need help and asking for help are two different things. Let's ask for help, we should not go through any negative situations on our own. A problem shared is a problem halved.

Having a sense of identity

"Knowing yourself is the beginning of all wisdom," Aristotle

"To be yourself in a world that is constantly trying to make you something else is the greatest accomplishment," Ralph Waldo Emerson

When we do not know who we really are, we have a tendency of allowing trauma to shape who we are or become. It often freezes us and stops us from recognising our strengths and harnessing our true power. Past trauma led me to lose my identity and to believe in the labels I was given as a result of what I have been through or was going through. I chose to break free from all the labels and embrace who God calls me to be. I refused to give power to the labels I was given as they limited me. Knowing our identity is very important, as it shapes our behaviour and creates the boundaries with which we live our lives. I hereby invite you to join me as we choose to be defined by the following:

- I am worthy
- I am sound and certain
- I make good decisions
- I am victorious
- I am fearfully and wonderfully made
- I am who God says I am
- I am fearless and courageous
- I am victorious
- I am more than a conqueror

- I am not defined by my past
- I am not defined by my environment or current circumstances
- I am destined for greatness
- I am light
- I am love
- I am an epitome of peace and joy

VICTORY AT LAST

Whatever we have been through life that didn't crush or kill us implies we have had victory over the situation. We must always keep in mind that we are victors and never victims of our hardships and setbacks in life. Everything happens for a reason, and if we are patient enough and willing to learn, we would be able to harness the treasures from our pain and hurt and be transformed, not victimised.

We all have good and bad moments in life. People with a victim mentality feel as though bad things keep happening to them and that the world is against them. Some people, when they go through bad moments, claim that it is not their fault, they blame other people or circumstances and they have no control over the bad situation. Any efforts to create change will fail, so there is no point in trying.

With everything that I have gone through, I had every reason to validate my victim mentality, but I decided to embrace my inborn ability to recover and thrive. I had power over my mind. What you give power to has power over you if you allow it. I had every reason to continue to blame my past and to feel pleasure when I received attention or pity as a result of what I went through. No one has power over your mind and life. No one should be given power to control our destiny. We are victorious, we are more than conquerors, and we can do all things through Christ who strengthens us.

Moving by Purpose not by sight

"Life is never made unbearable by circumstances, but only by lack of meaning and purpose," Victor Frankl

"Above all be of single aim, have a legitimate and useful purpose, and devote yourself unreservedly to it," James Allen

A person who has purpose in life has something to go for. Our purpose should pull us towards the future. As a visionary woman, you are not immune to the challenges, chaos, and disappointments of life. You will always face a lot of challenges, but you have to remain steadfast, tenacious, resilient, and hopeful. Our purpose must be powerful and clearer for it to pull us through all kinds of challenges and difficulties. We should not be swallowed by the challenges. Purpose helps us to remain focused and resilient when we face hardship.

We must refuse to be moved by what we see, as whatever we see is not permanent. Challenges and disappointment will always be there - let us not allow them to break us down or derail us from walking in our God-given life purpose. When life pushes you to the ground, force yourself back up. We learn from the challenges and use the lessons to propel us to our future.

Our vision and purpose should drive us towards our goals. The problems we face happen for us and not to us. If problems happen for us, we grow from them and be better, we must embrace challenges and thrive from them. In life, God allows us to walk through difficult paths for us to fulfil our life purpose and be the best version of ourselves. We can make lemons from lemonade. Regardless of problems we must remain true to our principles, values, and vision for us to walk in our God-given life's purpose.

That is why you must never give up, no matter what! You are a victor and not a victim, and remember, many have walked the path you are currently walking, and others will walk the same path in the future… Reach out and seek help if you feel lost or hopeless, and use the lessons learned to guide those who will walk behind you! Together we are powerful and can win every battle and conquer the world

CHAPTER NINE

STORY OF A LIFE

By Dr Bertille Nganwa

As a student living in Italy, I never imagined how much people's life experiences could affect their lives once they suddenly step into a new role, such as being a student, wife, professional, parent, manager, or leader.

It's obvious that our personality ethics are affecting every step of our lives.

I left Cameroon for Italy in 1996 to follow my dream of becoming a pharmacist and being a significant expert in bringing solutions to health matters in my country.

I was excited to leave my childhood place for another country. At that time, travelling abroad was a luxury. The ITALO-CAMEROON organization was giving scholarships to students who were admitted into the program and who successfully passed the Italian language exam.

The trip to Italy was very organized and it was an occasion to have new friendships.

Nevertheless, the years in Italy were challenging because I had to learn a foreign language for my studies. After staying in Italy and obtaining my degree, I had to go back to Cameroon because in between the years I got into a civil and religious marriage to Mr Nganwa, who resided in Cameroon for professional reasons.

1. Life in Italy

During my university years in Italy, I had to face several challenges, the first challenge being the completion of my university studies within the deadlines set for the Pharm. D. in pharmaceutical sciences with its hyper-loaded study programs. The second challenge was ensuring the proper growth of my first son, who was born when I was in my fourth year of university, with me still having two more years to go.

I remember the long trips I made to leave him at his daycare facility before going to my university and the mental calculations I made to find the right formula for picking him up after school at the end of my classes. All the while, I was doing a frantic race to get to the two infrastructures which were diametrically opposed to each other, and I had opted for a strategy that allowed me to leave the home where we resided with a stroller where I had comfortably installed the little one. I made the journey on foot for his school, and I did my best to leave home as early as 6am to give me the time needed to walk from home to the daycare facility. There, my bicycle was parked, which I then used to go to the university by juggling through the bike paths at a speed that was sometimes unmeasurable in order to reach the faculty in time to not miss any of the classes.

Visionary Woman

I had fought with the Italian jurisdiction that did not accept to accommodate a student with a child on its premises since it was not prewritten in the university texts, and I had the merits for having completed my exams of the first two years with excellence and still had an academic average that could see me enter the Table of Merits.

In my attempts to challenge this university law, which prohibited access to university lodging (although deserving), I was put in touch with a charitable association that helped me with the entire process. I eventually overcame this battle. My first great victory that greatly increased my faith. I was reassured that God always leans on the side of desperate cases, especially when a mother and child are involved.

To me, this was a little proof that the woman is the mother of humanity and her problems automatically become humanity's problems.

If you asked me to tell you where I got my strength to do all the things I did while being at the same time a student with endless hours of classes and exams of an enormity worthy of a Pharm. D preparation, then I would say I had a will of steel. I was more than focused on my studies, and somewhat obsessed about being one day called a Doctor in Pharmacy.

The laboratory sessions to carry out endless analyses on chemical mixtures of all kinds had taught me one thing about life: mixing two or more chemical substances under certain conditions like temperature and atmospheric pressure would always lead to a chemical reaction, the nature and outcome of which would depend on the way the process had been set up; Thus, I understood early on that whatever the situation we go through in our life and whatever the events we have to face, the way we manage them matters, if well managed, we will end up with a favorable or unfavorable outcome, and even if this outcome was not favorable, the lessons that would be drawn from it would be very important for the continuation of our earthly journey.

******

One day, as I was coming out of a rather exhausting exam, I had to run to pick up my son from school. I was very late and I had asked one of his supervisors to work overtime to wait for me. It was a winter evening and it was snowing hard, and when I finally arrived almost an hour later, I got to the daycare and saw my son and his supervisor were left alone, because all the parents had already gone to pick up their children except me.

I was very disturbed to have given additional work to the daycare that day, and in winter at that. Already aware of all the advantages that I was receiving with the special care that the entire team of this daycare was giving to my son, whose dad was in Africa and only had his mom, still a student, to take care of him. When I arrived, I was quite worried that my son had to be left alone without his crib mates for one more hour.

Alas, I was very surprised to find the little guy sitting quietly in his stroller sucking on his pacifier which almost never left him. Seeing me arrive all exhausted, he welcomed me with his amazing smile that I have always loved since the day he was born.

Visionary Woman

With that, I had just passed another test of life, which taught me the power of patience and to always keep my cool regardless of the situation.

My son had just given me a beautiful life lesson with this smile, whereas the situation could make anyone believe that he should have been crying upon my arrival. And this kind teacher didn't mind my being late and instead thanked me for having allowed her to spend an exceptional hour with my son, and also for having learned a lot from him during that hour, because he showed great patience and didn't worry about anything.

During my travels in the city of Ferrara, Italy, where we had become stars without knowing it, I was sometimes intercepted in the street by passers by simply to congratulate me and to admire my son.

I dreamed of my defense in pharmacy just like a newly wed's dream of getting pregnant .

I dreamed of the graduation ceremony and walking down the red carpet with my big card in hand and my son playing the best man.

Having been a wife while I was still a student had convinced me of what a marriage of two educated people who share the same goals but are forced to live apart for professional and other reasons could be.

I was convinced that a well-educated woman was better able to face the difficulties of a married life than a woman with little education.

I was aware that, being both a woman and a human being, I had to choose what was best for my life as a woman; that is, to study at university. I did not evaluate how difficult this higher education would be, nor how I was to blend this to my married life and the distance. However, I knew one thing, I had to do everything possible to achieve my life and career goals.

Always putting God at the forefront of all my choices has been my greatest spiritual victory. Yes, the Lord is at the center of my expectations and he guides my steps. I have often had to spend nights crying because I was so worried about my son and myself in a foreign country, very far from my family. I have spent sleepless nights praying and crying and, in the morning, I always had the strength to wake up, get out of bed, and face the reality of my life.

*****

After my graduation, I was faced with the difficult decision of immediately returning to my country without exercising my profession in Italy. How could this be possible since I had already fought hard to finish my studies and now, I was faced with the problem of employment and the second problem of family reunion. I never imagined I would have to solve such intense problems in my life. Faced with these facts, I simply had to take my destiny into my hands and give myself another reason to start over.

*****

After having hesitated on returning to Cameroon immediately after obtaining my degree in pharmaceutical sciences, I had in mind to put my knowledge to good use by working a few more years in Italy as a pharmacist before returning to my country.

This dream was becoming difficult to achieve, because the struggles I had faced in the past, those of finalizing my studies and being able to return to Cameroon to meet my husband were still ongoing, and I had no other way out than to return in order to lead a normal family life.

Even though I had the possibility of working in Italy, I still did not have the necessary support to do so: how could I continue to live as a single woman with a child in my care and be able to carry out my profession as a pharmacist!

*****

2. Life in Cameroon and its realities

Upon our arrival, the welcome was amazing, but I was concerned about starting a new life and integrating in my country. The years spent in Italy had certainly changed my mentality, the fights I had had hardened me, and I was sure that I could not please many people, because the financial means which I lacked were an obstacle to my development and my integration.

I realized that there is nothing more detrimental to someone's happiness than not being able to manage their daily life due to the lack of financial means.

I definitely needed to find a job in this world wherein I still needed adaptation from me and my worries, which were numerous.

I had to relearn how to live as a family because for almost two years after my marriage, I had not lived with my husband; the distance had taken its toll on our relationship and today we had to relearn how to share our daily lives together.

The hardest part was that there were no longer just two of us, but four.

I had had a second son immediately after the end of my studies and

I had taken advantage of the fact that I was preparing my definitive return to Cameroon to give birth to this second son in Italy as well.

It was a beautiful return, crowned with success: a good degree in pharmacy, and two children. It often happens that it is in the latter stage of life that we learn from what we have lived and even dare to say it and write about it.

*****

I soon readapted to life in CAMEROON and participated in activities that allowed me to reconnect with the reality of my environment by taking part in professional programs like seminars organized by pharmacists in my country.

I have also been a member of two associations of women. We met every weekend, during which I was able to reconnect with my compatriots and some of my childhood friends.

There was always something new to learn about how much people change as they grow older. While attending those seminars, I

Visionary Woman

quickly observed that everyone has his or her own style of engagement, probably because of the difference in mindset and point of view. The truth was that life in Cameroon was totally different from life in Italy.

******

The family responsibility was too much. Little money was at the center of the charges, Family member's expectations from what I could offer them were high.

I was in search of a job to be able to take care of my children. I had two little boys of mine and other family members and nephews to care for.

At the same time, I intended to restore to my mother the wealth and prestige that she had lost after my father's death.

My father was a hard-working man, who spent his entire life working so hard to secure a living for his family. We were a big family, and after suffering from Alzheimer's that weakened his health over the years he disappeared one day, without ever coming back.

When I was about to graduate, he was very proud of my progress and was very excited to be part of my graduation ceremony.

Until I had begun gathering all the administrative documentation to allow him to come to Italy, he left home one day for our village, telling my mother that he will be back very soon to collect all the documents needed for their departure to Italy; And never coming back. My graduation was mixed with this event, but nevertheless, I never allowed this tragedy to get in the way of my graduation.

******

NELSON MANDELA said, "In this life every man has twin obligations, obligations to his family, to his parents and children, and an obligation to his community and his country."

My family obligation was a priority and took time from my community obligation. I was family-centred and this attitude didn't help me enough in building a strong professional attitude. Being a housewife, taking care of my home, and my happiness was a choice I made, with the knowledge that this would limit me financially.

There were times when I turned down opportunities to get a good job as a pharmacist somewhere in the city, and so I always went for part-time jobs because I needed more free time for managing my home and family.

Every opportunity to work like a pharmacist was a great opportunity to express my knowledge and to be in tune with what I have sacrificed many years of my life. I spent seven years in Italy earning my doctorate degree.

Sometimes I felt so busy and trapped in the many roles in my life: pharmacist, house wife, mother, and so on. But the reality was that managing my own life and professional responsibilities made me more proud.

Everybody has the responsibility to be all that they can be for their family, for the world.

Mine was clear, because it takes too much energy to be what you don't like. I quickly discovered that when somebody is on the right track with themselves, there is an enormous energy inside them to inspire and heal, to let them pursue and achieve their dreams.

My husband is a hard-working man, and very ambitious. He finds himself in the category of those men who will put work and honor before anything else; having been raised by strict and demanding parents.

We needed to get to know each other again after years of life marked by distance. The realities of life in Africa and the feeling that some privileges accompanying our respective merits and social positions would be useful for a start. I had very quickly learned to live with enormous restrictions to ensure the survival of my marriage.

Human beings are not necessarily born in the same place they occupy later in life, and everyone should be able to use their intelligent faculties to fulfill their destiny and improve their lives.

Marriage is no different from a voluntary partnership where all the leadership would rest with one partner while the other partners would be required to obey orders. When choosing to marry, a woman should not automatically choose to live under her husband's orders, even if he kind of holds a better professional position than his wife.

Similarly, it would not be desirable for a woman not to take care of the management of her home because she wants to have a good professional career. In life, it is necessary to know how to make choices, because the children have only one childhood and if the parents are not present to cultivate a good education in them because they want to devote themselves to the professional work in order to provide for the needs of the family and to have a successful professional career, the consequences of such an abandonment of responsibility will be felt later.

*****

The Importance of Adapting in Life

Adaptation is a mandatory phenomenon in order to integrate into a new environment.

An environment will change as quickly as the people in it move: it is the law of nature.

How do you explain that some Africans, who have lived for a long time in the West, have difficulty reintegrating when they return to their native country! Yet this environment was theirs.

After several years spent outside my country, it was obvious that changes would have been felt in the relationships with others who were still back home. We know how different people's temperaments are depending on their own life history, their experience, and their ability to react to changes.

The world has evolved exponentially, new technologies have taken over, and everything that is lived elsewhere is now accessible on social networks.

When I came back in 2002, the use of social media was not as amplified as it is today. Social networks were not yet widely used by the Cameroonian population, so the myth of Europe was still an obsession for many people in Africa.

I fought hard to reintegrate and make my way. Sometimes I suffered defeats, other times I cherished victories. My family has been through many of my trials and tribulations in life, and while at times I thought I couldn't take it anymore, I started to get interested in other things.

I understood that I had to rebuild myself in order to quickly give a meaning to my life.

I learned a lot from other women: the visionary women's movement was a textbook case for my succession, I was interested through the power of social media on what was happening in other countries, how women living with daily difficulties had managed to give meaning to their lives: by helping other women to see clearly and to take charge of themselves.

Not everyone can be taken care of by everyone; it takes people with certain life experiences to inspire others to take care of themselves.

The Fundamental Role of Clarity in Success

Charity among women is a fundamental element to help other women have a better perspective of their life choices.

Charity must be based on three things:

1. Self-respect

2. Self-control

3. Personal work on oneself

Having to first of all work on yourself takes time, but this work, if well done, allows you to understand yourself and to give the right directives for your life as a woman.

It comes to mind that I should deal with the issue of women's rights in this last part of my story.

*****

For a long time, the recognition of certain women's rights has been a topical subject, despite the multiple fights led by feminist movements to grant women all over the world the solution to their multiple problems and injustices they face because of their sex.

In addition to the many rights they have, it is necessary to recognize the right of women to dream and the right to realize their dreams.

Why does the woman dream? And how can society help her realize her dream?

To realize her dreams, it is necessary that society recognizes her right to dream.

In a couple, the husband is considered the head of the family; he is the one who gives the main orientations and the directives to be followed by the couple and this is for the good of the family in general.

However, as the head of the family, a husband must be able to know the expectations of the members of the family, especially those of his wife.

Visionary Woman

Too often the woman deprives herself of the right to dream and deprives her children of the right to have a better future, because a woman has to expect everything from the husband by being satisfied with the role of housewife. It would not be possible to evolve beyond this already constraining task for the woman in order to aspire to the best that society could offer her.

The burden of household work and daily life falls on the mother, even when she has a job that keeps her out of the house for hours, the responsibility falls on her to find a way to adapt this job to the management of her household. She will often resort to a housekeeper who will cost her part of her salary.

The husband, being aware that his wife's contribution to the household will be useful for the management of his household, must be able to assert his status as head of the household so as not to leave the wife alone to manage the household; he must be able to team up with her. Unfortunately, this situation is often lived in an uncomfortable way by the African men, who would rather give themselves the freedom to become useful outside their house, and to indulge in other types of distractions.

Having a man who can take the lead in managing the family, running projects in parallel with his job to increase his family's income and for the sake of his family would be ideal for many women.

Society has granted advantages to men over women by facilitating them in the exercise of certain jobs with the aim that being the man, the head of the household who is one responsible for the family, it was necessary to grant him these advantages.

However, what society has forgotten is the fact that, in a given family, although the man is the head the woman is the administrator, and if this function is not attributed to her, many families will fall into jeopardy. This is one of the reasons for the degradation observed in many African families.

If one were to calculate the sum of the daily tasks that women have to face every day to ensure the smooth running of their home, blending household chores with the job outside the home, a well-organized couple will therefore be perceived as a solid team that should elaborate the rules of its internal management taking into account all visible and invisible aspects of its existence.

It had happened to me too often to make many choices, among which I had opted for the choice of deprivation; I deprived myself of a lot of things just to advance my dreams.

I had spent the first years after my final return to Cameroon working hard in pharmacies throughout the city of Douala; I had to accumulate hours of work in several pharmacies to be able to constitute savings to commence my project.

I dreamed of being a landowner and a business owner, a business which I still had in my well-buried dreams.

In 2004, after two years of hard work and having integrated a women's movement to participate in a tontine association, I was able to save money and acquire a piece of land in the PK15 district in

Douala, my city of residence. That was when the realization of the project LA VILLA VERTE MB materialized. So I will be pleased to present you its contents, although it is still in the process of finalization.

The financial challenge in Africa has opened the way to this quest for capital based on tontines. Women are the biggest beneficiaries because the purpose of tontines is to develop the spirit of saving within the communities in order to be able to grant members credit.

*****

Conclusion

By realizing a dream, the woman realizes a life project.

This contributes to giving her value and personal esteem. She holds a preconceived notion of being the master of her destiny.

In the multitude of roles that she embodies throughout her life, she is not only destined to be the bearer of life but much more. She should be destined to be the one who accompanies and guides her life partner and also the one who carries the destiny of a nation with an aptitude and grace worthy of her natural feminine power.

Conclusion

"Do not conform to the pattern of this world, but be transformed by the renewing of your mind. Then you will be able to test and approve what God's will is—his good, pleasing and perfect will."

Romans 12:2

As you read through the final pages of this manuscript, I urge you to let go of whatever narrative or identity you have been given or held up to this date, especially if they are negative and disempowering. Even though you cannot always control what happens to you or what people think of you or how they see you or identify you, you nevertheless have the potential and power to control the way you respond to what happens to you and what people do and say about you. You also have the power to set the pace and determine your destiny, not people or circumstances and chance. You may not always be able to tell people to treat you in a certain way or not to call you certain names or undermine or label you before they do so. However, you must not conform; you have the ability to choose and hold on to the way you want to be treated, identified, and called and to respond the way you want to when they treat you in ways that you disagree with.

Yes, you might have gone through some horrible things in your past. You might have been abused, you might have been a drug addict, and you might have been ... you name it ... yet, no one has the right to use these facts against you or to define you. Those were circumstances in your life; those were moments of your life that were needed to be pruned and shaped into becoming all that you were destined to become. Just like gold has to go through a hot furnace to be purified and become pure, you need to go through some of those challenges to bring out your best self and fulfill your life's purpose.

There is only one narrative you should hold on to concerning your identity, and this originates from your source, from the originator of life, your life. You are born and destined for greatness, to have dominion over all things and circumstances, including all that you are going through right now or will ever go through in your lifetime! Go now and start living a life of purpose and greatness. Go on and unleash your authentic identity. I wish you a wonderful and thrilling journey of self-discovery and unlocking your unique purpose.

Maybe, growing up as a child, your parents might have put you down, abused you and told you that you were of no worth. Please! You need to take off that belief. That is what they believe about you; that is not necessarily what you should believe about yourself because, like I said earlier on, the ideal person to speak to about a product is its manufacturer. The ideal person to give the final say about you is your

Creator, the Almighty God, and His final statement about you is that you are beautifully and wonderfully made; you are unique; you are destined for a purpose; you are a winner and not a loser; and it is in your Creator's best interest that you succeed because when you succeed, His brand succeeds and is trustworthy. You are created in His image. So your success is fundamental.

I want to tell you that this is who you should be looking up to, not another man; not your spouse; not your friends; not your neighbours; not even your teachers or your parents. They do not know who you are.

Have a dream…a vision, hold on to it…go to bed every day with a dream, and wake up each morning with a perfect purpose.

It is not how others see you that really matters in life…

It is how you see and perceive yourself that is important!

Others may see you as a tiny and powerless cat, but you see yourself as a mighty and courageous Lion! That is what is important and what truly matters! Go for it, believe in it, value the Lion within you. Change your thoughts, words, and perceptions about yourself, and start acting in ways that are in harmony with your true and most authentic self.

Change the way you see yourself…see yourself from the inside out, because you are the only one with the ability to see yourself this way…For only you know what your values, thoughts, and beliefs are…and others can only see and know about these qualities when you start speaking about them, writing about them, and acting in ways that complement them.

It is not what others think about you that really matters in life...

It is what you think about yourself that is important and really matters. As a man thinketh of himself, so he is...period! I rest my case, beloved!

It is not how others value and respect you that really matters in life...

It is how you value and respect yourself that is important and really matters...The value and respect you place and show to yourself determines your worth, and the value and respect others will place and show to you respectively...It's all right if some people still cannot value and respect you despite the worth and value you place and show to yourself...not just everyone can appreciate and value certain things and people in life... for three simple reasons:

1. They don't even know what value and respect mean
2. They can't appreciate and value themselves,
3. They suffer from very low self-esteem, low confidence, and an identity crisis...and simply will not accommodate those who are confident and secured in themselves and identity...In this way, they try to talk you down or pull you down to make themselves look bigger and taller...forgetting they have not grown, nor have you stopped growing or retarded in growth.

Finally...It is not what others believe or do not believe about you that really matters in life...

Visionary Woman

It is what you believe or do not believe about yourself that is important and really matters...For you could never go beyond the limitations and barriers of your own beliefs...

Your beliefs are the core and true source of your identity and image! They are the foundations that keep you firm and unshakable even in the midst of great storms and hardships...They are the roots that penetrate deep into the ground and keep you rooted and well-nourished... determining how big, strong, and firm a tree you can become...Those roots will determine how resistant and unmovable you become in times of the great storms and droughts.

If you must transform your life today, then I urge you to go back to the foundations...the roots...Go back to your beliefs, review them, uproot them, and change them if need be...or simply strengthen them...let them not be superficial...for you will be blown away by the most tender of winds...You will not be able to withstand the storms and droughts of life...

What are your beliefs...your convictions...if you don't know them, then you don't know who you are! Remember this "your beliefs become your values, your values become your thoughts, your thoughts become your words, your words become your actions, your actions become your habits, your habits eventually become your destiny.... Change your beliefs now if you must change your destiny...

True and permanent change must only come from within...

The beginning of true and permanent transformation begins with knowledge...knowledge and understanding of who you are, where you come from, why you are here, the greatness within you, etc. If only you could be still...look within you, and become aware and truly understand who you are, the great light and love that resides within you... then you don't need to search further...The light and love you search elsewhere is right within you and dwells in you...It is there to shine and illuminate all areas of darkness in your life and that of others...it is there to be exploited in your darkest hours...when clarity and light is needed to move forward without stumbling...

Are there any areas of darkness in your life you are struggling with? Are there still areas where clarity and light is needed to move forward?

Remember...Darkness is not an existential reality...it is simply the absence of light...Even during the darkest hours of the night, wherever and whenever there is light, the darkness ceases to exist...it becomes non-existent and unreal...

So today...where there is darkness in your life, family, relationships, etc, don't go trying to eliminate it by fighting it or questioning why it invaded your privacy or space...don't go trying to drive it out, rebuke, or bind it...don't go around crying and being sad and depress...simply reach out for the light...simply go where there is light...and the good news is, you don't have to go too far for the light...

Search for the light within and overcome darkness... You are light to the world.

Woman, Thy Seed Shall Be Great!

You are blessed and privileged to be called and chosen by the Almighty God and Creator of the universe to be the sole vessel through which every single man and woman on planet earth must be nurtured and led into the world! Great men and women of all calibers have been conceived, nurtured, and led into the world by you...and you continue to do so! Arise woman... Arise female child... Acknowledge your worth... Acknowledge your value... Be empowered in your rightful place! Your world needs you... Your sons and daughters need you. You must have a vision for your world... for your sons and daughters... for without vision, the people perish! The vision is more important than the visionary. We have come to leave a legacy for our children and the generation to come...what an honor and privilege. Join us now!

You are born to thrive... you are born for greatness...and no one but you can stop you from achieving greatness and fulfilling your purpose...your seed shall be great! You are a victor and not a victim, regardless of what you are going through at the moment. Your mess is your message to the world... to bring about transformation to those going through similar situations in life...and your pain...the power of your purpose...it ignites that burning desire and passion within you to initiate change...change not only for yourself but for all those in similar situations.

Arise and soar to greater heights like an eagle, because you are one!

As you read these final words, do not just put this book away and move on with your life… Let it serve as a roadmap you can always turn to for clarity, guidance, assurance, and hope when you are uncertain, challenged, troubled, worried, or even lost.

God bless you!

Authors' Biography

Dr. Sylvia Forchap-Likambi

Dr. Sylvia Forchap-Likambi is a visionary, multi-award-winning empowerment and transformation authority as well as a leading transformational speaker and six-times international best-selling author. Dr. Forchap-Likambi specialises in the delivery of very high-quality, cutting-edge empowerment leadership and transformation programs. She is the Founder and Global Chair of The Global Visionary Women Network, Founder and CEO of "Behaviour Changed," and Award-Winning Community Interest Company, Voice of Nations, and Global CEO and Consultant of Dr Sylvia Likambi International Health & Wellbeing Clinic. She is also the co-founder of Likambi Global Publishing.

Over the years, she has coached, empowered, inspired, and positively impacted/ transformed over 1.5 million lives globally, thousands of female entrepreneurs, and relentlessly empowered many to come out of addictions, depression, get into training, volunteering, employment/self-employment, leadership roles; and also offered them several of such opportunities through her organisations.

She grew up in Cameroon and later moved to Italy where she earned a Doctor of Pharmacy degree as well as a PhD. She was awarded the Italian Ministry of Higher Education and Research Scholarship for Excellence, and the Australian- Europe Scholarships to accomplish a year's collaboration with the University of Sydney (Nepean Hospital). Upon the completion of her Ph.D. in Australia and Italy, she worked as a postdoctoral researcher in Italy and the UK, and became an Honorary Research Associate with the Royal Liverpool University Hospital in 2008. She also became a member of The European Haematology Association in 2009. Sylvia has actively participated in leukaemia research and is an author and co-author of numerous international peer-reviewed journals.

She is also an ILM Certified Executive Coach and a Business and Life/ Mindset Transformation Coach.

She was awarded the Honorary Award for Exemplary Professional Leadership Recognition at the Enterprise Minds Awards 2018, the Positive Role Model for Gender Award at The UK National Diversity Awards 2016, and was a finalist multiple times for the Mentoring Champion of the Year at The SEN Powerful Together Awards 2012-2014 and The Member's Choice Awards in 2012 and 2013 (which celebrates the achievements of an individual who can demonstrate their commitment and contribution to the world of social enterprise, and how they have enabled entrepreneurs to achieve their goals).

She brings a very unique and dynamic blend of inspiration, purpose, empowerment, and transformation into her mentoring, coaching, and engagements, which has the potential of transforming the most dormant or negative mindset into a highly productive and positive one, capable of achieving any life goal.

She is a strong believer in the fact that as leaders we are called to serve rather than being served, and that to whom much is given much is expected. As a result, she endlessly embarks on a selfless journey of service and giving back to her community without the expectation of being financially rewarded or praised. Her greatest reward is in the satisfaction she gets from experiencing lives being transformed as a result of her humble service to humanity.

Her ethnicity, life experiences, educational background, resilient nature, and down-to-earth personality have given her the tremendous opportunity and privilege to serve and interact with some of the most deprived and underprivileged within diverse cultures, educational backgrounds, and communities; inspiring and challenging them to step forth confidently to unleash their untapped potentials and fulfil their dreams, regardless of their background, gender or circumstances.

She has also delivered several successful and life-transforming revolutionary leadership, empowerment, and business programs for VON (leading it to earn the prestigious SEN Behaviour Changed Award in 2013), WEA, HSBC, and a host of commissioned projects nationally and internationally. She has been featured on several national and international Radio and TV stations, to speak on the theme of female empowerment, entrepreneurship, leadership, and other topics; and has been a keynote speaker to several audiences, ranging from schools and community groups to universities.

Dr Sylvia Forchap-Likambi et al

For more information on Dr Sylvia Forchap-Likambi visit:

www.voiceofnations.org.uk

http://www.drsylvialikambi.com

www.globalvisionarywomenn.org

http://www.likambiglobalpublishing.com

http://www.littleangels-foundation.org

Dr. Anikphe Oyedeji

Dr. Anikphe qualified as a medical doctor in 1994 and is trained as a general physician and transplant nephrologist. Over the years, she has practised in Nigeria, Ghana, the United States of America, and the United Kingdom. She is currently involved in missionary work in northwest England.

Dr Anikphe Oyedeji currently lives in northwest England and works part-time in North Wales as a Consultant Physician at the NHS. She has been married for 20 years to Dr Ade, an Ordained Minister of the Gospel of Christ. Their purpose is to build the Body of Christ through apostolic teaching into fullness of maturity in Christ so the church is ready to welcome the return of Jesus Christ as King into the next age, his millennial reign. Together for 12 years, they have planted a local church in Ellesmere Port and ran the New Creation Centre, a community outreach project. She is a mother of four amazing children whom God has given her the privilege to develop as His gifts to the world. For the past 12 years, she has also co-owned a franchise care-at-home business. Life has been full to the brim. It's been a tough act, juggling so many balls and trying not to drop many, but His grace has been more than sufficient. Anikphe readily admits that it is a balancing act living out these various roles as co-labourer of Christ, career woman, mother, home-builder, and business owner while holding on to one of her main aims in life, which is to do all things with excellence and to the glory of God. In her contribution to this book, she shares her life-building story and her life journey so far, including low points and high points. She especially shares her story from the angle of how the promises of God and the Word of His Grace have been supernaturally sufficient. Her story lets us into God's handiwork in building her into the visionary and purposeful woman that we see today for His glory. But He is not done yet; her aim is to become God's fully mature and developed masterpiece.

Dr. Elizabeth Fon

Born on the 28th of August 1958 as the first born of 10 children to a primary school teacher and his home maker wife in the North-West region of Cameroon.

In form 3 while in the St Bedes secondary school, she plucked up courage to do physics since it was more or less a confirmed fact at the time that girls had to do domestic science to become good housewives while the boys did physics and mathematics to become engineers and doctors. Leadership came knocking early in her life when in form 4, she was appointed the lone Senior Prefect (SP) for boys and girls in a mixed college, ¾ of whom were boys. The boys felt slighted and started planning a strike action. However, in a few short weeks, she convinced the boys that she needed them as her team mates and they worked with her to the end of form five without any conflicts.

She has always done things that she was told only boys should do. That paved the way for her to develop a different mindset on how to interact and work with males in leadership roles because some years out of medical school, she had to head an all-male theatre team in the Bonassama District hospital in Douala.

As the first female DMO (District Medical Officer) of the Bonassama/Djebale/Cap Cameroon health District, she had to lead male colleagues across the Atlantic high sea to control health epidemics on the islands.

All of the above constituted adequate preparation for her when she was appointed the Littoral TB/HIV control program chief, coordinating the activities of 200 nurses/doctors/support staff in 39 treatment centre's where about 6,000 TB/HIV patients receive healthcare a year. That gave birth to the TESHO-Team Spirit Holistic program with a mission to teach life skills for stress reduction in Work/Life Balance. She has co-authored two books with her husband; "A Great Husband for a Great Wife" published in 2014 and "RECONCILE? NO WAY! to be released soon.

Born in a remote village, through the grace of God, she has evolved into a female leader who listens to people and meeting people's needs so they can experience their best life ever is more rewarding than silver and gold.

Angela Preston

Angela is the Founder and CEO of AP Coaching and Mentoring Services Ltd, a 3X International Bestselling Author, Radio Presenter/Playwright, and an award-winning Leadership Coach and Motivational Speaker for the UK. She is also a TEDx Speaker.

She is passionate about empowering others through her workshops and engaging talks. She is a recognised authority on confidence and personal development and regularly shares her expertise with radio and television audiences. She is the Founder of Angela Preston Coaching, which aims to coach business owners and entrepreneurs in setting and accomplishing their goals.

As an award-winning speaker, Angela has built her coaching, speaking, and writing business from scratch, earning her the respect and admiration of others for how she has not only overcome adversity but used it as a stepping stone to achieving her goals.

Before embarking on her entrepreneurial journey, she had experience in Leadership as a top-performing strategic manager, a role that has given her 20 years of hands-on experience within sales and management, leading teams of development managers and agents to achieve business goals, and taking one location from the bottom half of the company to number one in eight weeks.

Neva Brooks

Neva Brooks is the Diamond Sharp Certified Life Coach, Founder, and CEO of Diamond Sharp Coaching, LLC. By supporting professional, creative women, we navigate from the conflicts of life to places of confidence, freedom, and clarity. Neva is also a Registered Nurse and walks the journey of clarity with Nurses, especially during this unprecedented time for those in the healthcare industry. She leads Diamonds Sharpens Diamonds™, a women's support ministry. Through this ministry thousands of socks are donated to women and children in shelters and schools. This initiative is affectionately called "Sock It To Me."

Licensed and ordained as a Minister in the Christian Faith, Neva can be found expounding upon and teaching the concepts, and precepts of the Holy Bible. One of her passions, and assignments from God, is preaching the Gospel of Jesus The Christ. She is effective in presenting women's workshops, an accomplished conference presenter, and keynote speaker. She is a US Army Nurse Corp Veteran and serves as a Christian Medical Missionary in Lima Peru, South America, and Ghana West Africa. Here's a fun fact: She loves officiating destination weddings!

She has earned BSN, BSBA, and MBA degrees as well as multiple certifications in the Mental Wellness and Business fields. She is a published author, poet, and contributor: "Riley in Memoriam" Poets of Indiana, "Centered in Christ, Steadfast and Immovable" Devotional Volume 1; "Transformation YOU" Magazine, Dr Claude Dangerfield. Soon to be released Ghana 2022 Testimony and Prayer

Journal and The Visionary Woman: Moved by Purpose and Not by Sight.

Ellen Mandizvidza

Ellen Mandizvidza is a Registered Nurse, Entrepreneur, and an Empowerment and Business Start-up Coach. She is passionate about empowering women and girls to be financially literate and free, and she is currently working on becoming an accredited Financial Coach.

Ellen is also the visionary Founder and Director of Kharis Recruitment and Road 2 Success Academy.

She strongly believes that nothing can stand in her way of achieving her goals and fulfilling her God-given purpose.

By drawing lessons and wisdom from her own traumatic past, Ellen passionately shares her ground-breaking strategies to empower women and young girls to overcome challenges and build resilience.

Through her company, Road 2 Success Academy, she's committed to restoring hope in the hopeless by leading them through the path to achieving their dreams and becoming successful.

Blanka Volna

Blanka Volna is a visionary leader with over five years of experience in IT and finance. She is a first-generation ex-pat from the Czech Republic who has found her path by trial and error. She is also the proud owner of the Be Free With Blanka healing hypnotherapy practice. She helps her clients heal their physical issues and illnesses by understanding and releasing their past beliefs and memories. She loves to teach others and lead by example, breaking down complex problems into smaller manageable chunks and step-by-step processes.

Blanka has overcome many issues, such as dissociation from her body through dancing and physical activity. The girl who used to be clumsy and chubby and was once told that she couldn't run or was not an athletic type now spends at least three days a week at the gym or her dance and spin classes. Blanka is a firm believer that no matter your circumstance, you can change your life, and she is always open to having a conversation about goals, visions, and dreams. Be it in her practice or over an oat milk latte at her favourite coffee shop.

Blanka is also a Rapid Transformational Therapy (RTT) Hypnotherapist and Coach.

Thelma Birchall

Thelma Birchall is a wellbeing coach and an accredited nutritionist registered with the Association for Nutrition. She is deeply passionate about coaching and empowering people to live healthy lifestyles and experience great health and well-being.

She is a visionary leader, wife, and mother of four beautiful children.

Thelma obtained her Bachelor's degree in Health, Wellbeing, and Nutrition (Combined Honours) at Liverpool Hope University. In 2017, she completed and obtained her Masters in Public Health Nutrition at Liverpool John Moores University.

Thelma has worked in private, public, and community settings as a well-being coach and nutritionist, and has several years of experience working with adults, children, and people with disabilities. Her key areas of focus to transform her clients' wellbeing are nutrition, diets, and physical activities, all of which are linked in with healthy living.

With her non-judgmental approach to food, diets, nutrition, health, and life in general, she naturally attracts people of all walks of life who seek her counsel and mentorship in many ways.

Dr. Bertille Nganwa

Dr Bertille Nganwa graduated from the University of Pharmaceutical Sciences in Ferrara, Italy, in March 2002. She is the visionary Founder and Director of VILLA VERTE MB. Dr Nganwa is also the Regional Director and Vice President of Voice of Nations, Cameroon, and the Africa Chair of Global Visionary Women Network.

After having worked as an assistant pharmacist in a Cameroon-based pharmacy for two years, she takes the orders of "pharmacist – Replacente" and became manager of another pharmacy in the city of Douala, Cameroon.

From 2006 until 2010 she worked for a pharmaceutical company where she was responsible for the pharmaceutical production of solutes to quality control and packaging of solid forms, capsules, and tablets in large manufacturing units, until the sector was closed in 2010. Dr Nganwa then returned to teaching until 2016, before embarking on a pioneering health project and founding VILLA VERTE MB, following her accumulated years of professional experience and knowledge.

About the Publisher

Published by Likambi Global Publishing Ltd.

We are a Dynamic Family-Led Cutting-Edge Global Publisher set up to simplify and enhance your writing and publishing experience and unique journey to becoming a renowned and confident author.

Whether you are an adult or a child, we have a bespoke package and special team that is devoted to working with you throughout your writing and publishing journey with us!

All of our consultants and coaches/ mentors are best-selling authors with years of hands-on experience and a wealth of knowledge uniquely tailored to meet your individual needs!

Our goal is to provide you with the ultimate writing and publishing experience required to share your unique message and voice as an author with the world and strive to greater heights and platforms!

Publications are done three times a year, in January, June and November.

All manuscripts must be received at least 90 days prior to publication dates.

Likambi Global Publishing Contact Details

Website:

www.likambiglobalpublishing.com

Email:

enquiries@likambiglobalpublishing.com

Address:

208a Picton Road, Liverpool, L15 4LL

United Kingdom

www.ingramcontent.com/pod-product-compliance
Lightning Source LLC
Chambersburg PA
CBHW050022130526
44590CB00042B/1724